THE GRACEFUL GENERATION

DR. Willibroad W. Ticha

Copyright © 2023 by Dr. Willibroad W. Ticha

All rights reserved. No part of this book may be used or reproduced by any means, graphic, electronic, or mechanical, including photocopying, recording, taping, or by any information storage retrieval system, without the written permission of the publisher except in the case of brief quotations embodied in critical articles and reviews.

Contents

Introduction 1

Chapter 1: The Privilege of Knowing God's Will 3
   A Chosen Generation 3
   Why We Can Know God's Will 5
   We Are Gods 7

Chapter 2: The Humanness Of Our God 9
   The Feeling That Someone Cares 9
   A Caring High Priest 12
   Our Only Condition 15

Chapter 3: The Accessibility of God By All 16
   The Old Covenant Pattern 16
   The Temple Setting 17
   The New Covenant Pattern 19
   God's Plan of Redemption and Restoration 20

Chapter 4: All Things Work For The Good
   Of The Saints 23
   Embracing Challenges in the Ministry 28

Chapter 5: God Works In Man To Will And To Do 31
   How God Quickens Us to Will and to Do 33
   Nothing to Boast of Ourselves 36
   The Only Condition 38
   The Role of God's Law Inscribed in Our Hearts 39

Chapter 6: Freedom from The Law 41
    What a Topic 41
    The Relevance of the Law 42
    Impossible to Live by the Law 45
    God's Wisdom about the New Nature 46

Chapter 7: Understanding The Word Of Grace 49
    Rightly Dividing the Mystery of God's Grace 49
    Humility is Acknowledging and Confessing 54
    Wake-up, Church 55
    No One is above Scriptural Authority 57
    When Peace Finally Comes 59

Chapter 8: The Line Drawn By Grace 60
    Grace is not Cheap 60
    The Demands of Grace 61
    1. Live in Purity 62
    2. Continue in the Faith 63
    3. 'All or Nothing' Rule 65
    4. Walk by Knowledge 68

Chapter 9: The Dangers of Grace 70
    The Abuse of Grace 70
    How to Know When Grace is Abused 71

Chapter 10: Provision of a Door of Escape 77
    God's Grace in Temptations 77
    The Expected Mindset of the Christian 78

    Characteristics of Temptation 80

    How Not to Yield to Temptation 82

Chapter 11: Reinforcing The New Covenant 86

    Transitioning to the New Covenant 86

    The Focus of the Minister 87

    The Ministries of Death and Righteousness 89

    Dimensions in Grace 90

    The Strangeness of the New Covenant to Angels 91

Introduction

Dearly beloved, we are living in a very dynamic era ever in the history of humankind. This is the era of God's grace. The truth about the manifestations of God's grace in this generation is something others in ancient times were not privileged to experience.

I pray we understand that we are living in the most privileged era in the history of the church. An era in which success is certain to whoever desires, thirsts, and gravitates towards it, especially the desire for a greater intimacy with God. This is because the grace of God has greased the path making it much easier for the accomplishment of the desired goals. The truths within this book points us to the fact that there remains no excuse for failing.

What makes this generation dynamic is the fact that in everything people set out to do for the LORD, He goes ahead of them making all crooked paths straight. He then goes in them to facilitate their efficiency, and effectiveness so that the results that were expected will be realized.

It is rather unfortunate that many individuals have despised the grace of God, and rather treat it as a reason to compromise Christian virtues and values, as well as their commitment to the work of the ministry. This is because God by the expression of His grace, seems to be gentle, tolerant, slow to anger, etc.

But in this book, we will equally examine the dangers of abusing God's grace to all those who take it for granted.

Dear reader, as you go through this book, I pray the light of God's word on this subject of His grace will shine more in your spirits, and will bring such illumination in your heart that will enable you to soar beyond the storms of life as an eagle. God bless you.

Yours in His Service,
Dr. Willibroad W. Ticha
Defender of the Faith

CHAPTER 1

The Privilege of Knowing God's Will

A Chosen Generation

It is important to note that there has never been a generation as privileged as this present generation. The scripture clearly affirms this: *But ye are a chosen generation, a royal priesthood, an holy nation, a peculiar people; that ye should shew forth the praises of him who hath called you out of darkness into his marvelous light: Which in time past were not a people, but are now the people of God: which had not obtained mercy, but now have obtained mercy. (1 Peter 2:9-10)*

From this text, one can see that this is a chosen and peculiar generation, a kind that has never existed. Its peculiarity is not only in terms of the era and times in which it appears in God's apocalyptic calendar, but more so because of the terms and uniqueness with which God interacts and deals with us in this era, which is much different from His interactions with the ancients. The scripture emphasizes that we are a peculiar people that have now been privileged to be considered as sons and daughters of God in deed:

"Behold, what manner of love the father hath bestowed upon us, that we should be called the sons of Gods... beloved, now we are the sons of God." (1 John 3:1-2)

"But as many as received him (Jesus), to them gave he power [the right] to become the sons of God, even to them that believe on his name." (John 1:12).

The people of the Old Covenant were not considered as sons of God, not even those who loved the Lord. Those that loved and served Him were considered as servants of the Lord. As such, being servants, they were not given the privilege of knowing the will of their Master. But we have that privilege, as sons. God has called us of the New Covenant to 'show forth His praises.' This distinguishes us from the Old Covenant (Old Testament) believers. Adding to this distinction, He again emphasized in Deuteronomy 10:15 that; *Only the LORD had a delight in thy fathers (those of the Old Covenant Era) to love them, and he choose their seed after them, even you (those of us of the New Covenant Era) above all people, as it is this day.* Realize that He simply loved our fathers (the ancients of the Old Covenant), but He didn't choose them. Rather, He chose their seed after them, which we are.

The benefits and privileges of this chosen generation is only for those who are born-again, that is, those who have responded to His calling of them to step out of darkness (the world and sin) into His marvelous light: *"And the disciples came, and said unto him (Jesus), why speakest thou unto them (the multitude of unbelievers) in parables? He answered and said unto them, because it is given unto you to know the mysteries of the Kingdom of heaven, but to them it is not given." (Matthew 13:10-11).*

> You only benefit from the Lord when you respond to His instructions.

This is proof that unbelievers are not part of this chosen generation since they are not privileged to know the will of God: *But the natural man receiveth not the things of the Spirit of God: for they are foolishness unto him: neither can he know them, because they are spiritually discerned. (1 Corinthians 2:14).* You only benefit from the Lord when you respond to His instructions. This lack of knowledge of certain spiritual realities was not only about the unbelievers, but also of most of the Old Testament saints: *"Whereby, when ye read, ye may understand my knowledge in the mystery of Christ, Which in other ages (i.e. Old Testament) was not made known unto the sons of men (for the scripture didn't even call them sons of God' for they had not that privilege to be sons of God which we do have today), as it is now revealed unto his holy apostles and prophets by the Spirit." (Ephesians 3:4-5)*

As evidently portrayed, being privileged to knowing the will of God is a general phenomenon for present day saints of God. This privilege was not only restricted to Paul, but to all, as it is now revealed unto His Holy Apostles and Prophets by the Spirit.

Why We Can Know God's Will

For what man knoweth the things of a man, save the spirit of man which is in him? Even so the things of God knoweth no man, but the Spirit of God. Now we have received, not the spirit of the world, but the Spirit which is of God; that we might know the things that are freely given to us of God." (1 Corinthians 2:11-12)

We immediately see that the reason why we can know God's will is because we have the Spirit of God living in us. This started the day we got born again, as that was when the Spirit of God came and took His abode in us. This is an experience which unbelievers do not have, neither does the Old Testament saint, as the Spirit of God was not living in them. He could only come periodically upon the Old Covenant saints to enable them to perform particular tasks. (See Judges 16:1-20).

And just as it is only a man's spirit that knows the secret things that belongs to him, so also, only the Spirit of God knows the secret things of God. Therefore, by reason of Him dwelling in us, He reveals to us God's secrets. What a treasure and opportunity for greatness! No doubt the Scripture is true as it says: *Eye hath not seen, nor ear heard, neither have entered into the heart of man, the things which God hath prepared for them that love Him. But God hath revealed them unto us by His Spirit, for the Spirit searcheth all things, yea, and the deep things of God in (1 Corinthians 2:9-10).* John the apostle also testified of this when he wrote, *"But the anointing which ye have received of Him abideth in you, and ye need not that any man teach you: but as the same anointing teacheth you ALL THINGS, and IS TRUTH, and IS NO LIE, and even as it hath taught you, ye shall abide in Him." (1 John 2:27)*

> The primary conditions to keep on knowing the will of the Father is by continuing to abide in Him, avoid grieving the Spirit through disobeying His instructions, and a constant walk in holiness.

Hence, the primary conditions to keep on knowing the will of the Father is by continuing to abide in Him, avoid grieving the Spirit through disobeying His instructions, and a constant walk in holiness. Knowing His will for us per time, will help us to know how to plan our daily activities and how to go about them. James had this to say about knowing God's will: *Whereas ye know not what shall be on the morrow... For that ye ought to say, if the Lord will, we shall live, and do this, or do that. Therefore, to him that knoweth to do good, and doeth it not, to him it is sin. (James 4:14, 15, 17).* This means we are held accountable if we know God's will and do not act as expected —His will becomes our assignment!

> We are held accountable if we know God's will and do not act as expected —His will becomes our assignment!

It thus leaves us with no doubt that knowing God's will because of His Spirit dwelling us is quite a privilege. This definitely distinguishes us from previous generations.

We Are Gods

The Scriptures are clear on us being gods, and places us at a point of dominion, rulership, governance, and authority in the terrestrial realm. We are to exercise our dominion and governance, just as God does in the celestial realm: *"Love has *been perfected among us in this: that we may have boldness in the Day of Judgment; because as He is, so are we in this world." (1 John 4:17).* Since the Spirit of God in this dispensation dwells within us, that thus makes us gods: *I have said, Ye are gods; and all of you are children of the Most High. (Psalms 82:6).* What a treasure! A 'Chosen Generation' indeed — because of God's grace (unmerited favor) towards us as a result of Christ sacrifice on the cross for us: *"Blessed be the God and Father of our Lord Jesus Christ, who has blessed us with every spiritual blessing in the heavenly places in Christ, just as He chose us in Him…having predestined us to adoption as sons by Jesus Christ to Himself, according to the good pleasure of His will…by which He made us accepted in the Beloved. In Him we have redemption through His blood…" (Ephesians 1:3-7).* Congratulation fellow reader, the grease is already on your elbows!

CHAPTER 2

The Humanness Of Our God

The Feeling That Someone Cares

Certainly, one of the most peaceful emotional strengthening, and comforting feelings in the heart of adversity when everything else seems to be falling apart is the feeling that someone cares. That gives hope to the hopeless, and puts a smile on the face of the distressed, as they learn to press on with life no matter the circumstances. Though David passed through such depressing situations, he encouraged himself in the Lord: *Yea, though I walk through the valley of the shadow of death, I will fear no evil: for thou (God) art with me; thy rod and thy staff they comfort me. (Psalms 23:4)*

> The road to success is always under construction. (Anonymous)

What a great assurance to have that God is always by you. That is the point in which instead of crisis breaking the individual, it rather gives him every reason to be positive, with high expectations for a turnaround. The road to success is always under construction. If David though living in the Old Covenant era was that positive, even when the Holy Spirit was not yet freely given to mankind, how much more should we be positive and conscious of the Lord's presence with us, who live in present times of grace, and since God now resides in us. — *For our bodies are the temple of the Holy Spirit. (1 Corinthians 6:19)*

> **Theodore Roosevelt, the 26th President (1901-1909) of the U.S. once said, "No one cares how much you know until they know how much you care."**

Unfortunately, there are quite a good number of people in our society today who have never experienced the love of someone who cares. Theodore Roosevelt, the 26th President (1901-1909) of the U.S. once said, "No one cares how much you know until they know how much you care." This is an indisputable evident that everyone gravitates towards love. Love is indeed more powerful than knowledge — Knowledge without love is opposed, but love without knowledge is appreciated. Think about the aborted or abandoned babies who will never experience the love of a mother. The Bible emphasize

> **Love is indeed more powerful than knowledge —Knowledge without love is opposed, but love without knowledge is appreciated.**

the importance of love: *Can a woman forget her suckling child, that she should not have compassion on the son of her womb? Yea, they may forget, yet will I not forget thee. (Isaiah 49:15).* Also *Psalms 27:10: When my father and my mother forsake me, then the LORD will take me up.*

It is comforting to know that God's attachment to us is even beyond what a breastfeeding mother may show to her suckling child. He has promised never to abandon us nor be distant from us, and that the assurance of His ever presence with us should form the basis of our boasts and confidence in Him: *Let your conduct be without covetousness; be content with such things as you have. For He Himself has said, "I will never leave you nor forsake you." So we may boldly say: "The LORD is my helper; I will not fear. What can man do to me?" (Hebrews 13:5-6)*

This demonstrates how favored and chosen we are. God is so concerned about us in this generation and has made provision for His grace to operate in us due to the sacrifice of Jesus Christ on the cross. God had a covenant with His Son Jesus Christ, on the basis of His shed blood, to protect us who have believed in His Son, and to bring us to a perpetual life of victory. Consequently, any accident, calamity, sickness, etc. befalling you is either doing so illegally, or you granted it permission by not believing and not standing on what the shed blood of Christ accomplished for you. It is time to awaken to the reality of the privilege the cross brought to you, and resist all such works of darkness confronting you. Rebuke it and do not allow it come near you or dominate you, for God's covenant of protection is upon your life. John affirms to this when he wrote in *1 John 4:4, You are of God, little children, and have overcome them, because He who is in you is greater than he who is in the world.*

A Caring High Priest

Hebrews 4:14-16 says, Seeing then that we have a great High Priest, that is passed into the heavens, Jesus the Son of God; let us hold fast our profession. For we have not an High Priest which cannot be touched with the feeling of our infirmities; but was in all points tempted like as we are, yet without sin. Let us therefore come boldly unto the throne of grace, that we may obtain mercy, and find grace to help in time of need.

What a great treasure! Before Jesus Christ gave Himself as a sacrificial offering (ransom) for the redemption of mankind, the throne in Heaven was not called the Throne of Grace. It actively acquired that name after Christ's sacrificial offering to purchase the eternal souls of lost mankind. In the Old Testament, the Mercy Seat was a type or a figure of the New Testament reality, Throne of Grace. That was why in the Old Covenant, the blood of animals would be placed upon the Mercy Seat, signifying the yet to be accomplished sacrifice of Christ. But in the New Covenant, the Son of God became the sacrifice.

> **In the New Covenant, there is no other seat in heaven called the mercy seat apart from Jesus Christ — He is our mercy seat!**

With the eternal wounds of the crucifixion and the freshness of the blood on the wounds, He is seating on the Throne. Therefore, qualifying the throne as the Throne of Grace. This is because His blood does not cry out for judgment, nor for justice against the sinner, rather, it cries for mercy and grace, justifying and interceding for the repentant sinner. His blood speaks better things than Abel's blood — that cried judgment against Cain (Hebrews 12:24). In the New Covenant, there is no other seat in heaven called the mercy seat apart from Jesus Christ — He is our mercy seat! Rather, there is the Throne of Grace, on which He presently sits. He has now become the embodiment of God's mercy and grace.

Jesus Christ, our great High Priest, is greatly touched by our infirmities, as He always intercedes for us: *Wherefore he (Jesus Christ) is able to save them to the uttermost that come unto God by him, seeing he ever liveth to make intercession for them. (Hebrews 7:25).* We know that His intercession for us is powerful and effective, knowing that He is not only touched by our feelings, infirmities, weaknesses, or even sins, but also that He Himself suffered while on earth and experienced all that which can plague the human soul. But in it all, He remained sinless: *"Who (Jesus Christ) in the days of his flesh, when he had offered up prayers and supplications with strong crying and tears unto him that was able to save him from death, and was heard in that he feared; though he were a son, yet learned he obedience by the things which he suffered." (Hebrews 5:7-8)* Also, we read; *"For in that he himself hath suffered being tempted, he is able to succor them that are tempted." (Hebrews 2:18)*

We must take note, else we misunderstand the Scriptures and think that His sufferings and perhaps temptations were the results of His foolishness or some wrong things He did. No!

These were challenges He was subjected to during His earthly journey. He humbled Himself and went through all these for the purpose of redemption of all who were slaves to sin: *And being found in fashion (in appearance) as a man, He HUMBLED Himself, and became obedient UNTO DEATH, even the death of the cross; (Philippians 2:8).* Due to this great work of our High Priest Jesus Christ, our repentance from sin was accepted and we were justified as guiltless. We thus have the boldness to approach the *Throne of Grace,* demanding for mercy and grace at any and every time we need it. Genuine repentance and brokenness of spirit when we falter qualifies us for His grace and mercy. For He said a broken heart and a contrite spirit He will not despise (Psalms 51:17).

This privilege is available whenever you need it as the Scriptures emphasizes —*find grace to help in time of need.* Hence, you are not left alone, neither forsaken, neither condemned, because of the graceful and caring heart of our High Priest. Such a privilege was never so in the Old Testament. For them, He was more of a 'consuming fire' at the face of acts of unrighteousness: *"For the LORD thy God is a consuming fire, even a jealous God." (Deuteronomy 4:24).* But today, the administration of His wrath is much different. He does not punish us immediately, rather, He gives us the time to repent so His grace will declare us not guilty. He convicts us by His Spirit to run to Him with a repentant heart, as He does not want to harm us: *"For such a High Priest became us, who is holy, harmless, undefiled... and made higher than the heavens." (Hebrews 7:26)*. It is our continuous refusal to repent that eventually bring us to experience His wrath.

Our Only Condition

There is only one condition that we need to meet in order to ensure a continual flow to us of this great work of unlimited grace of our High Priest. *Hebrews 10:21-23: And having a high priest over the house of God; Let us draw near with a true heart in full assurance of faith, having our hearts sprinkled from an evil conscience, and our bodies washed with pure water. Let us hold fast the profession of our faith without wavering; (for he is faithful that promised).*

The condition is, we must be sincere before Him with a true heart, sprinkled from an evil (sinful) conscience, and our bodies (spirit, soul) washed with pure water, which is the truth of His word. As a result, even when we mistakenly falter, His intercessory work will avail for us, and His blood will automatically cleanse us from all iniquity, as we call on Him. What a favored generation! It almost seems as though God is chewing our food for us, so we can just swallow; *For through Jesus (our great High Priest), we both have access by one Spirit unto the Father. (Ephesians 2:18)*

CHAPTER 3

The Accessibility of God By All

The Old Covenant Pattern

Looking back at the Old Testament, you discover that God did not make Himself known to everyone at the same time. He chose to go on with specific individuals at specific periods. When it was the time of Moses, it did not matter how spiritual Joshua was, God would not reveal Himself to him. It was until Moses died that the Scripture revealed that God spoke to Joshua for the first time: *"It came to pass that the LORD spoke to Joshua the son of Nun, Moses' assistant, saying: 'Moses My servant is dead. Now therefore, arise, go over this Jordan, you and all this people…as I was with Moses, so I will be with you…'" (Joshua 1:1-5)*.

Also, when it was the time of Elijah, no matter how righteous Elisha was, Elijah was first taken to Heaven before God revealed Himself to Elisha. It happened almost exactly this way for all the Old Testament prophets and those that succeeded them. It was a little different with the case of Eli and Samuel. Eli was still alive when God approached Samuel. God bypassed Eli to Samuel:

"And the LORD came and stood, and called as at other times, Samuel, Samuel. Then Samuel answered, Speak; for thy

servant heareth. And the LORD said to Samuel, Behold, I will do a thing in Israel, at which both the ears of every one that heareth it shall tingle. In that day I will perform against Eli all things which I have spoken concerning his house...For I have told him that I will judge his house for ever for the iniquities which he knoweth; because his sons made themselves vile, and he restrained them not." (1 Samuel 3:10-13)

Reading the entire story, you will discover that, from the day the Lord approached Samuel to talk to him, God called Samuel three times, but Samuel did not know it was God since he was never acquainted with God's voice, though he prayed to Him daily. God had never revealed Himself to him prior to this time. God kept calling, but He would not even call Eli so he could coach Samuel to realize it was God calling him. This implies God had already rejected Eli as priest before Him. That was why He then turned to Samuel. Hence, the Lord kept using Samuel and He never used Eli again as priest before Him until He killed him. This affirms to the fact that in the Old Covenant, God functions with specific individuals at specific epochs and only would reveal Himself to others after the death of His servants.

The Temple Setting

The Old Covenant temple had three different sections: the outer courts, the holy place, and the Most Holy place. The entire congregation stayed at the outer court, while the priest goes into the holy place where he burns incense to the Lord.

And once a year, the high priest (with a rope tied around his waist which extends to the outer court) goes to the Most Holy place, where the presence of God was. Only the high priest had the right to go into the Most Holy place to encounter God, as well as to offer sacrifices. Then he comes to the outer court to communicate to the people the message from the Lord.

This further confirms the fact that God related with specific individuals only and at specific times. If the high priest dies in the Most Holy place due to God's judgment, the people will pull him out by means of the rope that was attached to his waist. For no one else was permitted to enter the Most Holy place except the high priest. Anyone else who tried to get there would face the judgment of God, even being struck dead by the Lord.

The reason why God gave this restriction was because from the fall of man in Eden, man became unrighteous, and the blood of animals which were being offered for atonement simply covered sin, without totally blotting it. Sin could only be perfectly atoned for by the blood of the Lamb (Jesus Christ) which had not yet been shed then. God's presence would consume such an individual who dares to get into the Most Holy place. The high priest did not get consumed when he goes there because he was chosen by God for that, and he had on the priestly garment, which signified the righteousness of God —God thus sees him as righteous. The blood of the animal on the mercy seat, was symbolic of atonement.

The New Covenant Pattern

The New Covenant came with lots of privileges. When Jesus finally died on the cross, His blood atoned for our sins, and the curtain of the temple separating the Most Holy place from the holy place was torn supernaturally in two, from top to bottom. Thereby removing the restrictions as to the fact that only the High Priest could get in there once a year. The priest could make his way there as well, and not just once a year as the case was before, but at any time. Also, every other person who could only remain at the outer courts, were then made priests and kings, thereby qualifying them to be able to get into the Most Holy place: *"Jesus, when he had cried again with a loud voice, yielded up the ghost. And, behold, the veil of the temple was rent in twain from the top to the bottom..." (Matthew 27: 50-51).* We also read, *"But ye are a chosen generation, a royal priesthood..." (1 Peter 2:9).*

> No limitations nor restrictions as to who can be in the presence of God. The limitations we may face will be decided by our hunger for Him.

This implies we have all been called to forever leave the outer court into the holy and Most Holy places. Therefore, we all can (and should) have intimate relationship with the Lord without Him showing any favoritism of persons. No limitations nor restrictions as to who can be in the presence of God. The limitations we may face will be decided by our hunger for Him. We can experience His presence all the times. We do not have to go to the temple before we can experience His presence with us, for He made our bodies His temple (But going to fellowship with others is very necessary as His word commands us to). Hence, He made His abode in us: *"Or do you not know that your body is the temple of the Holy Spirit who is in you…" (1 Corinthians 6:19).*

God's Plan of Redemption and Restoration

From the fall of man in the Garden of Eden, man could no longer relate with God on one-to-one basis, for man was cut-off from fellowship with God as a result of sinning. That was why God had to come upon specific individuals at specific times, for specific purposes. His plan had always been to restore man to Himself, so they could again commune intimately on one-on-one basis. He technically worked out this plan through the course of history in diverse ways, till Jesus Christ was crucified, dead, buried, and then resurrected. His crucifixion was the perfect legal ransom for mans' redemption. Christ then breathed into man (His disciples) the Holy Spirit as He urged them to receive Him (John 20:22). From that time, God's technical plan for the full restoration of man was accomplished, as man acquired a better status than he had before the fall.

> The pride of being born again is that you are not only different from Adam, but you are favored and preferred more by God.

Before the fall, though God communed with them, yet, man was physically separated from God. Praise God, for in this generation, God lives in man. The pride of being born again is that you are not only different from Adam, but you are favored and preferred more by God. No doubt, when Satan and all the forces of darkness realized this technical plan of God, they in anguish regretted crucifying the Lord Jesus. Joel the prophet affirms to the fact that it was the long-desired plan of God to relate with each individual at all times: *"And it shall come to pass afterward, that I will pour out my Spirit upon all flesh…" (Joel 2:28).* Therefore, without any gainsay, the grace of God has appeared to all men in this generation (Titus 2:11). This grace appearing to all men is what John meant when he wrote: *"In him (Jesus) was life, and that life was the light of men…" (John 1:4)* Therefore, God's grace is demonstrated by Jesus Christ (through the Holy Spirit), indwelling all those who have received His offer of salvation.

We are indeed special, as the Old Testament saints did not experience this reality. This brings us to a life of no limitations. Paul the apostle made his boast on this when he said, *"I can do all things through Christ who strengtheneth me." (Philippians 4:13).* So, it now behooves us to occupy and exert our influence on the earthly realm as we focus on advancing His kingdom and reign over humanity. Christ speaking prophetically about this when He said: *"A certain nobleman (Jesus Christ) went into a far country (from Heaven to earth) to receive for himself a Kingdom (Bible says we are redeemed by Christ as a Kingdom of Kings and priests), and to return (ascension back to Heaven). And he called his ten servants (you and I), and delivered them ten pounds (talents or gifts as some translations put it, which implies the 'Holy Spirit' whom Scripture reference as the Gift of the Father. Jesus had prayed that the Father should give the Holy Spirit to His disciples), and said unto them, Occupy till I come." (Luke 19:12-13)*

Praise to God for His grace enables you to occupy till He comes. That is one of the major privileges you have in this generation, as opposed to the Old Covenant dispensation, to which Ezra the prophet reiterates: *"And now for a little space grace hath been shown from the Lord…" (Ezra 9:8)*. All the grace the people of the Old Covenant ever experienced was always for a little while, which was as a result of God's seasonal mercy for them. For us today, it's endless.

CHAPTER 4

All Things Work For The Good Of The Saints

It is important to note that the rebirth of the saints in Christ was not of the will of man or the flesh, but of God (John 1:13). God knows His plans for your life, and so, He knows for sure what to allow your way and what not to. He knows what you can bear and endure. Even though at times you might get overwhelmed and frustrated thinking He has abandoned you, His word assures us: *"For I know the thoughts that I think toward you, says the LORD, thoughts of peace and not of evil, to give you a future and a hope." (Jeremiah 29:11)*

> Many are not accustomed with challenges and trials. They fail to realize that every true destiny will be tried and opposed.

Never think that God is slow in fulfilling His purposes for your life. As it is the case with many, especially when they seem to be going through diverse challenges irrespective of His promises and prophecies of greatness for their lives. Remember Joseph who had dreams of greatness and rulership, yet, unexplainably, he began going through one disaster to the other. It is almost as though life and nature were against the realization of the divine dreams. Many in such situations have questioned whether the dreams were really from the Lord, while others have questioned the existence of God. This is so because many are not accustomed with challenges and trials. They fail to realize that every true destiny will be tried and opposed.

> In critical moments, all you need to do is to stay faithful to the Lord, focusing on the vision while upholding biblical ideals.

Joseph was thrown into the pit and later sold as a slave by his own brothers, accused of rape falsely by Potiphar's wife, sent to prison by Potiphar, and forgotten for two years in prison by a jailer whom he had once helped to interpret his dream. You can see that opposition came to him from strangers, friends, and family. That is when it becomes most frustrating, when even your loved ones seem to be the ones fighting your dreams. It can be understood and explainable when the devil and your enemies are the ones fighting you, but it is unbelievable when your opposition is from your own household. In critical moments, all you need to do is to stay faithful to the Lord, focusing on the vision while upholding biblical ideals.

With Joseph, it almost felt like God was slack and unable to fulfil His word to him. But a day came when God orchestrated a strategy for Joseph to find favor with the king, by giving the king a dream which no one could interpret but Joseph. As soon as he interpreted Pharaoh's dream, he was appointed ruler in Egypt, second in command to the king. Everything he once lost was fully recovered and he became the ruler he once dreamed of. God is very true to His promises toward us and the Scriptures cannot be broken (John 10:35). All the negative challenges that came to him on every side were now of the past. More so, to all those who accused him, he became greater than every one of them: *And we know that all things work together for good to them that love God, to them who are the called according to his purpose (Romans 8:28).* The story of Joseph and his later elevation is a shadow of the New Covenant saints. It tells of the glory they will experience if they endure hardships and opposition for the sake of their stand in Christ Jesus.

> **What slows the realization of God's promises in your life, is your inability to submit to His leadership.**

God is not slow concerning fulfilling His purpose for your life. Often, other than mere oppositions coming against you, what slows the realization of God's promises in your life, is your inability to submit to His leadership. Consequently, you go through certain unnecessary events that could have been avoided. Yet, in the midst of that, He is working a divine plan for your good as soon as you tend to Him in repentance. But there are events we cannot avoid, for they are part of the process to greatness.

Though Paul was called of God and separated from the womb by God to be His servant, yet, He went through situations in life that he eventually began fighting even God who had called him from his mother's womb. He entangled himself with the Pharisees (a wrong career), he partook in the stoning of Stephen a follower of Christ, persecuted the Church, and much more. Every passion of his heart was contrary to the destiny the Lord was calling him for. Later in life, after he had repented, he testified: *But when it pleased God... to reveal his Son to me, that I might preach him among the heathen; immediately I conferred not with flesh and blood, (Galatians 1:15-16).*

He was brought to trial before Festus the governor and king Agrippa, being persecuted for preaching the gospel by the Jews and the same Pharisees he once belonged to. He defended the course of his faith and said he was not disobedient to the heavenly vision of preaching Jesus Christ to the world (Acts 26:19). In fact, God is never late even when we are the ones opposing the realization of His plans in our lives. All He needs from us is repentance and the willingness to follow His leadings. It might seem time is far gone, but as you walk with Him in righteousness, He will quicken and speed up the realization of the dream —*For a quick work will the Lord do and cut it short in righteousness. (Romans 9:28)*

Solomon was right when he spoke such great wisdom by the Spirit of the Lord, captured in the experiences of his adventures: *To everything there is a season, and a time to every purpose under the heaven (Ecclesiastes 3:1).* Who could have believed that Paul the persecutor of the Church, would preach the Gospel and write about two-third of the New Testament, especially considering the extent of his persecution of the disciples. Also, the fact that he adhered passionately to their traditional practices (Galatians 1:14), made him more hostile to the Church, which is called to be different from the godless elements of the culture of the society. His conversion happened when he was on one of his trips to arrest Christians.

No doubt, when God finally saved him, he became very zealous after the gospel and he would not permit anyone to hinder his preaching of Christ, neither will he back-out because of the persecutions he was encountering: *"Let no man disturb me, for I bear on my body the marks of Christ. Paul indeed had a 180-degree turnaround." (Galatians 6:17).* God will always turn it all around for your good if you come back to Him. It does not matter how much bad you might have committed, if you still genuinely love Him, and have a true repentant heart, then, *"His Goodness and mercy shall follow you all the days of your life as you dwell in the house of the Lord forever." (Psalms 23:6)* This is also confirmed in *2 Corinthians 9:8, "And God is able to make all grace abound towards you; that ye, always having all sufficiency in all things, may abound to every good work."*

> God's promises are brought into effect only as you keep walking by His word and precepts.

God's promises are brought into effect only as you keep walking by His word and precepts. Backsliding from His precepts, both exposes and makes you vulnerable to the schemes of the wicked one: *"When a righteous man doth turn from his righteousness, and commit iniquity, and I lay a stumbling block before him, he shall die…" (Ezekiel 3:20).* The reason why the Lord has chosen to work out everything for your good, is because of His unfailing love toward you: *"The LORD hath appeared of old unto me, saying, Yea, I have loved thee with an everlasting Love: therefore with loving-kindness have I drawn thee." (Jeremiah 31:3).* In this dispensation of grace, the fullness of this love is demonstrated by Christ Jesus: *"For greater love had no man than this that a man lay down his life for his friend." (John 15:13). Jesus* came to the world based on the plenitude of the Father's love for mankind to be redeemed: *"For God so loved the world that he gave his only begotten Son, that whosoever believeth in him should not perish, but have everlasting life." (John 3:16)*

Embracing Challenges in the Ministry

So far, we have focused more on our private lives. One may begin to wonder about the challenges preachers experience in the ministry. As a preacher, once you are confident that your walk in the ministry is by the instructions and leadership of the Spirit of God, then, irrespective of the challenges you encounter, it will all work out for your good. Jesus made reference to this mindset when He faced oppositions in the ministry: *"The stone which the builders rejected, the same has become the chief corner stone: this is the Lord's doing, and is marvelous in our eyes." (Matthew 21:42)*

Let's examine one of such challenges Paul the apostle encountered in the ministry: *"Being confident of this very thing, that he which hath begun a good work in you will perform it until the day of Jesus Christ: Even as it is meet for me to think this of you all, because I have you in my heart; in as much as both in my bonds, and in the defense and confirmation of the gospel, ye all are partakers of my grace."* (Philippians 16-7)

In Philippians 1:9, 12-20, he says; *"And this I pray, that your love may abound yet more and more in knowledge and in all judgment... But I would ye should understand, brethren, that the things which happened unto me have fallen out rather unto the furtherance of the gospel; So that my bonds in Christ are manifest in all the palace, and in all other places; And many of the brethren in the Lord, waxing confident by my bonds, are much bolder to speak the word without fear. Some indeed preach Christ even of envy and strife; and some also of good will: The one preaches Christ of contention, not sincerely, supposing to add affliction to my bonds: But the other of love knowing that I am set for the defense of the gospel. What then? Not withstanding, every way, whether in pretense, or in truth, Christ is preached; and I therein do rejoice, yea, and will rejoice. For I know that this shall turn to my salvation through your prayer, and the supply of the Spirit of Jesus Christ. According to my earnest expectation and my hope, that in nothing I shall be ashamed, but that with all boldness, as always, so now also Christ shall be magnified in my body, whether it be by life, or by death."*

In these verses, Paul says a lot about the work of the ministry, his bonds, and the brethren. The way one embraces the challenges in the ministry determines whether God's objectives for the ministry will be furthered. Paul was positive when he faced challenges. He did not seek to save his life, but to profess the faith even at the detriment of his comfort and safety. It all turned around for the various good:

i. Despite the bonds in which he found himself, he prayed for the believers whose love for God and the work of the ministry abounded more and more in all knowledge and judgment.

ii. Despite the tribulations and the bonds, the way he approached it instead led to the furtherance of the gospel. It was while Paul was in bonds (chains) in prison, that he wrote most of the letters to the various churches. We are thankful to God for his zeal for the gospel, though he was in chains, for his bonds gave us two-thirds of the New Testament. It resulted to the good of the Church, and in all palaces and places. What about your own bonds?

iii. His courage as he faced his bonds and challenges by being relentlessly bold to preaching the gospel; caused many preachers to be birthed after his kind.

iv. It brought the body of Christ together as one, as they began communing concerning Paul. Paul said that he knows he will not be put to shame, for whether he dies or lives, Christ must be magnified in his body.

Beloved, whether in life or dead, God will turn it around for your good.

CHAPTER 5

God Works In Man To Will And To Do

There is no exaggeration in saying that it is not only a great privilege but also a wonder that God works in the heart of man both to will and to do of His good pleasure (Philippians 2:13). God does so for a couple of reasons:

First; because there is absolutely nothing good that can come out of man except by the Spirit of God indwelling him: *It is the Spirit that quickeneth, the flesh profiteth nothing: the words that I speak unto you, they are spirit, and they are life (John 6:63).* Paul also says in *2 Corinthians 3:6: Who also hath made us able ministers of the New Testament: not of the letter, but of the Spirit for the letter killeth, but the Spirit giveth life.*

Secondly; there is a breaking, humbling, consecration process that is activated in the heart of man when God begins to stir and work on his heart for service. The perfecting of God's work of consecration on the man's heart, qualifies him as a vessel of God fit for the Master's use. For God will not receive any service from a vessel with traces of sin, and pride:

Nevertheless, the solid foundation of God stands, having this seal: "The Lord knows those who are His," and, "Let everyone who names the name of Christ depart from iniquity."...Therefore if anyone cleanses himself...he will be a vessel for honor, sanctified and useful for the Master, prepared for every good work. (2 Timothy 2:19,21)

Thirdly; God will only be fully part of what He initiated and is at the head of the various processes for its realization. His divine nature will not tolerate an alternative; *"I am the Alpha and the Omega, the Beginning and the End, the First and the Last." (Revelation 22:13).* Jesus actually was making reference to this age-old truth when He said in *Matthew 15:13-14: "Every plant which My heavenly Father has not planted will be uprooted… They are blind leaders of the blind. And if the blind leads the blind, both will fall into a ditch."*

Also, the writer of Hebrew emphasized this concept when he made us to realize that any race we are running for the Lord, it must have been initiated by God for it to be of God, and as we run it, we keep our eyes on Him for instructions and coaching, to be able to finish well: *"…Let us run with endurance the race that is set before us, looking unto Jesus, the author and finisher of our faith…" Hebrews 12:1-2.*

Therefore, whatever you are to engage in for the Lord, you must be sure He is the initiator of it. Else, your labor, energy exerted, time spent, resources depleted, will all be futile. *Psalms 127:1* admonishes, *"Unless the LORD builds the house, they labor in vain who build it; unless the LORD guards the city, the watchman stays awake in vain."* Everyone would testify of your hard work, but there will be nothing to show for it.

How God Quickens Us to Will and to Do

As mentioned before, the truth of God's word coming alive in your spirit by the working of the Holy Spirit in your heart, is a key factor in the quickening process of the Lord, to make you to will and to do of His purposes: *For the words which I speak to you, they are spirit, and they are life. (John 6:63).* The word of God imparts life to your human spirit. It thus influences your spirit as it comes more alive in God's word, and begins to resonate with the frequency of God. It is almost as two different radio waves resonating almost at the same frequency, starts intersecting one another. You almost start hearing a different radio broadcast interjecting the channel you are tuned to.

> Your spirit begins to resonate with the Spirit of the Lord as you pray and meditate more on the word of God.

Your spirit begins to resonate with the Spirit of the Lord as you pray and meditate more on the word of God. That helps your spirit get more aligned with the Spirit of God. This intensifies to the point where your spirit is swallowed into the Spirit of God. This is what the Scriptures meant to be ever filled with the Spirit. It results in you desiring only what the Spirit desires. It is at this point that one hates iniquity and love righteousness, which is quite different from simply avoiding the acts of sin because the Scriptures commands us to. At this point, every desire and tendency to gravitate towards unrighteousness is killed.

The Lord desires all of us to attain this reality. Your own will disappears as your spirit is synchronized with His Spirit. In Gethsemane Jesus prayed that if it is possible, the Father should take away the cup of suffering He was about to drink from. But ended up the prayer by saying that His own will should not be done, but what the Father wills. He had come to the place where His Father's will was His natural habitat. He even testified that He could of Himself do nothing, but what He sees His Father do, that also He does (John 5:19). This would mean we get empowered on the inside by the Spirit of God to do that which the Lord wills: *"God did this so that they would seek him and perhaps reach out for him and find him, though he is not far from any one of us. For in him we live and move and have our being." (Acts 17:27-28)*

> When your will sublimes with God's will, then He can fully use you to declare His total counsel.

It is at this point when your will sublimes with God's will, then He can fully use you to declare His total counsel. Every godly passion in a man's heart (spirit), whether as to soul-winning, financing the advance of the Gospel, family, etc., came about either through prophecy, meditation on the word of God, or him being brought by the Holy Spirit under a particular spiritual atmosphere (impartation), or the Spirit presented to him a problem that his spirit became uncomfortable with, thereby, creating in him the desire to seek for the solution. Once the Lord has revealed His will to you, your spirit grasps it, and is set to prayers. That activates your spirit to the point the Revealed Will becomes like fire within you: *"Is not my word like fire," declares the LORD, "and like a hammer that breaks a rock in pieces?" (Jeremiah 23:29)*

The power of the revealed word breaks every hindrances in your heart and birth passion in you for the word. Jeremiah experienced this fire in his life, and became a preacher of the word, though he had refused the calling into the ministry under the pretext that he is a child, when the Lord first revealed it to him (Jeremiah 1:5-6). But the continual meditation of the word broke the hesitations to the Spirit of God and made him willing to do the Lord's biddings. Jeremiah became so passionate after the ministry of the Lord: *But if I say, "I will not mention his word or speak anymore in his name," his word is in my heart like a fire, a fire shut up in my bones. I am weary of holding it in; indeed, I cannot. (Jeremiah 20:9)*

As the word of God becomes real to you, you can not hold back, but go out to passionately execute the biddings of the Lord.

This is the quickening of the Spirit to do the will of God, by means of His spoken word revealed in your spirit. One thing you must realize is that it is not the mere written word (the letters i.e. The Logos) that quickens, but the spoken word (revealed word i.e. The Rhema) that the Spirit reveals to you for a particular situation. To say it another way, the Spirit behind the revealed word quickens: *"Who also has made us able ministers of the New Testament; not of the letter, but of the spirit: for the letter killeth, but the spirit giveth life." (2 Corinthians 3:6).*

Therefore, one man can read the Bible over and over, but never receives anything from it, neither gets imparted with passion for the Lord's biddings, as is the case with many. This is because they simply read it, but fail to give the Holy Spirit the time needed to work on their hearts and to make the word come alive. This could have been possible by dedicating considerable time in prayers as you meditate (pondering upon what you read). Then the Spirit of God will then begin to work on your heart transforming it as well as birthing His revelations in your spirit. This culminates in activating your spirit to do the Revealed Will of God.

Nothing to Boast of Ourselves

As seen already, nothing good can come out of us, if not by the Spirit of God working in us both to will and to do. Thereby, ridding us of every reason to boast. For to will and to do of His good pleasure is not of our making, but a demonstration of His grace to us: *"That no flesh should glory in His presence." (1 Corinthians* 1:29)

Further, the Scriptures say, *Not that we are sufficient of ourselves to think any thing as of ourselves; but our sufficiency is of God. (2 Corinthians 3:5)*

David cried to the Lord, *"Restore to me the joy of your salvation, and make me willing to obey you." (Psalms 51:12).*

Therefore, every exploit we will ever have will be to the praise of His name, irrespective of the efforts we put into it. Paul had a perfect comprehension of this, in both his personal life, and ministry engagements, *'It is no longer I who lives, but Christ living in and through me' (Galatians 2:20).* This is what makes living under the dispensation of grace formidable, as it does not depend on your struggles to live righteously. For man's righteousness is like a filthy rag before Him (Isaiah 64:6). It depends solely on His righteousness at work in us:

"But by the grace of God, I am what I am: and his grace which was bestowed upon me was not in vain: but I labored more abundantly than they all: yet not I, but the grace of God which was with me." (1Corinthians 15:10).

Now the God of peace, that brought again from the dead our Lord Jesus, that great shepherd of the sheep, through the blood of the everlasting covenant, make you perfect in every good work to do His will, working in you that which is well pleasing in his sight, through Jesus Christ; to whom be glory for ever and ever Amen. (Hebrew 13:20- 21)

> **Christ giving His life on the cross for man became the source of man's strength and empowerment.**

Wow! What a great privilege! All these because of Christ's sacrificial offering on the cross! His work on the cross was complete. This is what makes God peaceful towards this generation (the dispensation after the cross). Such an immeasurable grace —His work on the cross was exactly what the Father needed for the restoration of fallen man. Every time the Father thinks of His Son's sacrifice on the cross, such sinless and peaceful offering, His eyes flow with loving tears, His heart flows with unending love, mercy, and ceaseless grace, and His total being stretches out to embrace man. Christ giving His life on the cross for man became the source of man's strength and empowerment, to perfectly do the biddings of the Father. So, our boast is anchored on Him and for Him. Without Him, we are nothing.

Romans 11:16-18, "For if the first fruit is holy, the lump is also holy; and if the root is holy, so are the branches. And if some of the branches were broken off, and you, being a wild olive tree, were grafted in among them, and with them became a partaker of the root and fatness of the olive tree, do not boast… But if you do boast, remember that you do not support the root, but the root supports you."

Also, the prophet Isaiah speaking prophetically about this generation: *"Can a woman forget her nursing child, and not have compassion on the son of her womb? Surely they may forget, Yet I will not forget you. See, I have inscribed you on the palms of My hands; Your walls are continually before Me." (Isaiah 49:15-16)*

The Only Condition

The most important condition for the Holy Spirit to continue to work in us to will and to do of God's good pleasure, is for us to totally surrender our lives to His leading, and to comply with

His working in us: *"...He that abideth in me [Jesus] and me in him, the same bringeth forth much fruit; for without me ye can do nothing. If a man abides not in me, he is cast forth ...and is withered ...and they are burned. If ye abide in me, and my words abide in you, ye shall ask what ye will, and it shall be done unto you". (John 15:5-7)*

Abide in Christ and let His words abide in you, and the Spirit of God will never stop such a successful work in your life. What else could demonstrate the awesomeness of God's grace other than the fact that He works in us to will and do the good pleasure of the Lord.

The Role of God's Law Inscribed in Our Hearts

One thing that easily facilitates the working of the Holy Spirit in a man's heart to both will and do, is His inscribed laws in his heart. This forms the foundation of the inner witness of the Spirit. This is necessary to the man as he confront life issues, or as he listens to sermons. With that, he can judge the happenings around him, whether they are of God, and which step to take: *Indeed, when Gentiles, who do not have the law, do by nature things required by the law, they are a law for themselves, even though they do not have the law. They show that the requirements of the law are written on their hearts, their consciences also bearing witness, and their thoughts sometimes accusing them and at other times even defending them (Romans 2:14-15).*

The inscription of God's laws on the hearts of men was a phenomenon of the New Covenant. Whereas in the days of the Old Covenant, the law was inscribed on tablets of stone confined in the ark of the covenant, and kept in the Most Holy place. This inscription of His laws in one's heart makes it easier for him to be convicted, for the Spirit works in his heart to will and to do. His conscience bears witness to what the Holy Ghost wants done, and causes him to easily submit to the will and desire of the Holy Spirit.

CHAPTER 6

Freedom from The Law

What a Topic

The challenge of many Christians is how to live the Christian life in righteousness. Many have resorted to the conclusion that it is not possible to live righteously. And they blame it to the law, saying that it is difficult to keep the laws of God. Many have justified themselves in compromise quoting the Scriptures: *"There is none righteous, not even one." (Romans 3:10)* They misinterpret this Scripture, and have remained on that conclusion, hence, a life of sin.

So also, were my thoughts, until the Lord opened my understanding to the freedom from the law. The revealed truths brought my mind to a place of rest as I understood the demands of the law for righteousness was fulfilled in my heart. It empowered me and took away the fear of transgressing God's laws. Living the Christian life in righteousness should not be a struggle when you understand this. Living righteously should be a natural consequence as you acknowledge and receive the truth of His finished work of grace on the cross. Talking about the freedom from the law is in no way to cast a negative picture about the law, for the law is not evil. Rather, the law reflects the excellency of the nature of God.

The Relevance of the Law

The law itself is not bad, for Jesus declared in *Matthew 5:17*, *"Do not think that I have come to abolish the Law or the Prophets; I have not come to abolish them but to fulfill them."* Considering also the following Scripture: *Galatians 3:23-25*, *"But before faith came, we were kept under the law, shut up unto the faith which should after-ward be revealed. Wherefore the law was our schoolmaster to bring us unto Christ, that we might be justified by faith. But after that faith is come, we are no longer under a schoolmaster."* There are precepts and concepts of the finished work of Christ on the cross that unless we are granted understanding to its mysteries, the interpretation of the Scriptures will be heretical.

Paul the apostle revealed to us the grace he found with the Lord that he was granted understanding into the mysteries of the New Covenant, *"Surely you have heard about the administration of God's grace that was given to me for you, that is, the mystery made known to me by revelation…In reading this, then, you will be able to understand my insight into the mystery of Christ, which was not made known to people in other generations as it has now been revealed by the Spirit to God's holy apostles and prophets." (Ephesians 3:2-5)*

The good news is that anyone in this dispensation of grace, who will dare live a holy life and crave for a deeper walk with the Lord as he prayerfully searches the scriptures, will be granted an understanding of the depths of God's word.

A schoolmaster, was always a slave who was entrusted to accompany a family or a Jewish little child to and from school, guarding him, and ensuring his safety. When he accompanies the child to school, he let him go into the class to be taught by his classroom teacher. Once that was being done, the child was no longer under his custody or influence. As such, he will wait outside until they are through with classes, then accompany him home.

Therefore, a look at the above Scripture, it is evident that faith (Christ and His teachings) is compared to the work of the classroom teacher, while the laws compared to the schoolmaster. When the teacher was with the children, the schoolmaster had no control whatsoever over them.

This implies that the law helped us not to go beyond the boundaries of divine expectations for our lives. It ignited a fear of punishment if we did. That helped prepare our hearts so it will not be difficult to accept Jesus Christ. This reflects also on the approach in which most parents raise their children. As they are being taught values, discipline, etc., they grow in wisdom and maturity. They now know how to take care of themselves, and their safety. They then outgrow the need for their parents telling them what they have now understood is their responsibility. They can now manage their lives properly. Therefore, the responsibility their parents had to guide them on basic behaviors is now met in their lives. They now live by knowledge of the truth as to what is befitting of them. Likewise, us who have come to know Christ and have become one with

Him, we no longer live under the pressure of Dos and Don'ts, but the knowledge of the truth of who we really are in Christ, keeping with the standards of righteousness met in our lives.

For example, your teenage son brushing his teeth in the morning not because of fear of being scolded, but because he knows it is the rightful thing to do —that is living by knowledge. Therefore, he brushes his teeth not under pressure to obey the parents, but he happily does that first thing in the morning because it is the right thing. His new realities have now been defined. He now realizes the standard of cleanness is for his own good, as opposed to a burden his parents are placing on his shoulder. That is what God wants us to experience as He frees us from the Dos and Don'ts of the law, to a better way of life.

Hence, the relevance of law was to bring us to faith. Now that faith has come, you are no longer under the law, nor under the pressure of a series of rules and regulations of Dos and Don'ts. This in no way makes you above the law, neither does it annul God's laws, but it means the laws and its demands have been realized in your heart. It has become your normal, natural, daily, new nature reality in Christ. On the contrary, any man who feels he is under custody of any sort, always feels like rebelling —but you are a free man in Christ: *"It is for freedom that Christ has set us free. Stand firm, then, and do not let yourselves be burdened again by a yoke of slavery" (Galatians 5:1).* By this yoke of slavery, Paul actually meant the schoolmaster i.e. the law.

Impossible to Live by the Law

Matthew 23:1-4 says; Then spake Jesus to the multitude, and to his disciples, saying, the scribes and the Pharisees sit in Moses, seat: All therefore whatsoever they bid you observe, that observe and do; but do not ye after their works; for they say, and do not. For they bind heavy burdens and grievous to be borne. And lay them on men's shoulders; but they themselves will not move them with one of their fingers.

The scribes were the people who copied the laws in the scrolls (with their hands), while the Pharisees were the teachers of the laws. No doubt Jesus said they were seating on Moses' seat, because Moses did both. Jesus realized that what the Pharisees were teaching was not totally contrary to the laws — *Whatsoever they bid you, observe and do!* The reason why Jesus was always in disagreement with them was not even for the fact that they were not doing that which they bid others to, but because He came to properly interpret the laws, as He puts an end to the dispensation let by the schoolmaster, so that the grace dispensation could takeover. But the Pharisees will not let Him do that. Jesus called living by the laws a heavy burden, grievous to be borne, which the Pharisees were putting on the people, and could not carry it off the people shoulders with their tiny finger. By this, Jesus meant He wants to usher a new dispensation of grace that will enable the Christian life easier to be lived.

The Pharisees could neither observe the laws they taught, nor carry the burdens they placed on the people. This proves that it is impossible to keep the law by human efforts. Jesus implied the laws are great when He said He did not come to abolish the laws and the prophets, but to fulfill them. Therefore, His goal is to usher in a grace dispensation in which the laws which are difficult to be kept, could be meet in the hearts of men. This due to the new nature the believer have in Christ. *"Therefore, if anyone is in Christ, the new creation has come: The old has gone, the new is here!"* (2 Corinthians 5:17). Thereby, living by the standards of the law will no longer be a struggle as its demands have been met in the new creation.

God's Wisdom about the New Nature

The laws reveal God's nature. God giving the laws to man was not because He thought man could keep the laws, but it was showing man His expectations of him. Man knowing that he could not keep it by his own abilities, would cause him to realize the need for total reliance and dependence on God to meet those expectations. That sets the stage for Christ to step in, providing grace for man. But man first of all must deny self and surrender his will to Christ's. The surrendering, however, can only happen when man realizes that he died with Jesus on the cross and was raised to a new life as Christ was raised from the dead. This great wisdom of God to bring every one into a new nature in Christ Jesus was a strategy to get the standard of His laws fulfilled in man: *"Therefore, if any man be in Christ,* he is a new creature: Old things are passed away; behold, all things are become new." (2 Corinthians 5:17)*. He adds; *"For in Christ Jesus neither circumcision availeth anything, nor uncircumcision, but a new creature." (Galatians 6:1)*

God by His unlimited wisdom gave man a new nature in Christ, which is the nature of God and His laws, as He is one with His laws. This means, man no longer needs the law to tell him not to sin before he sees the need not to. Rather, through God's nature, he has come to naturally detest sin. For him to even be tempted to commit certain acts of sin, he needs to first develop lust towards it. Else, he cannot be tempted, just as God cannot be tempted: *'When tempted, no one should say, "God is tempting me." For God cannot be tempted by evil, nor does he tempt anyone; but each person is tempted when they are dragged away by their own evil desire and enticed. Then, after desire has conceived, it gives birth to sin; and sin, when it is full-grown, gives birth to death.' (James 1:13-15)*

No doubt, the Scriptures emphasize that in Christ Jesus neither circumcision (i.e. the law, for it was the law that brought in circumcision) avails anything, nor uncircumcision, but a new creature. That is, the struggles to keep the law or not does not yield any result, but a new creature. This is the confidence we have in Christ. *"As many as believed and accepted Jesus Christ, he gave them the power to become Sons of God." (John 1:12)*.

This new nature in Christ is the result of the sealing of the Spirit when we died with Christ on the cross and resurrected with Him to a newness of life: *"After that ye heard the word of truth …ye believed, ye were sealed with that Spirit of promise?" (Ephesians 1: 13)*. Being sealed with the Holy Spirit, and given a new nature in Christ, enables us to remain as God's children, enabling us to live sin-free: *"Whosoever is born of God doth not commit sin for his seed remaineth in him…" (1 John 3:9)* It is further reiterated: *"What shall we say, then? Shall we go on sinning so that grace may increase? By no means! We are those who have died to sin; how can we live in it any longer? Or don't you know that all of us who were baptized into Christ Jesus were baptized into his death? We were therefore buried with him through baptism into death in order that, just as Christ was raised from the dead…we too may live a new life… For we know that our old self was crucified with him so that the body ruled by sin might be done away with, that we should no longer be slaves to sin —because anyone who has died has been set free from sin." (Romans 6:1-7)*

CHAPTER 7

Understanding The Word Of Grace

Rightly Dividing the Mystery of God's Grace

It is the obligation of pastors and all those involved in teaching the gospel to understand what grace is. This is because it is the true revelation of God's grace that saves lives, as well as building them into Christian maturity and freedom from sin. Unfortunately, many have not been able to understand the reality of its simplicity, while others have made it complicated by stretching it beyond the canonicity of Scriptures. Their concept of grace now contradicts other biblical doctrines. Carefulness in handling the integrity of biblical doctrine is vital. James warned of this: *"My brethren, let not many of you become teachers, knowing that we shall receive the greater condemnation, for in many things we offend all. If any man offends not in word (word here is not in terms of speech as to grammatical errors, but in terms of revelation truths of God's word), the same is a perfect man, and able also to bridle the whole body?" (James 3:1-2)*

The strength and productivity of a person's spiritual life is a direct function of the teachings he has received. Many teachers do offend in doctrine because of:

> **The strength and productivity of a person's spiritual life is a direct function of the teachings he has received.**

i. Lack of proper training on biblical exegesis (unfolding of Scriptures).

ii. They want to impress their audience by teaching deep things.

iii. They have hidden objectives in their hearts as they present the word to the people —thereby corrupting the word (eisegesis —introducing their own opinions on scriptures).

iv. They do not take their devotional moments of prayers and Bible meditation seriously.

Paul cautioned Timothy about succeeding well in ministry, *"Until I come, devote yourself to the public reading of Scripture, to preaching and to teaching...Be diligent in these matters; give yourself wholly to them, so that everyone may see your progress.*

Watch your life and doctrine closely. Persevere in them, because if you do, you will save both yourself and your hearers." (1 Timothy 4:13, 15-16).

The Lord gave same instructions to Joshua about the carefulness with which he must approach the meditation of the Scriptures: *"Be careful to obey all the law my servant Moses gave you; do not turn from it to the right or to the left, that you may be successful wherever you go. Keep this Book of the law always on your lips; meditate on it day and night, so that you may be careful to do everything written in it. Then you will be prosperous and successful." (Joshua 1:7-8)*

> Until God and your devotional moments are treated with lots of reverence, understanding the word of God properly will be a witch-hunt.

We can see that a very key factor amidst others in understanding the Scriptures, is to meditate on the Scriptures always (all seasons: day and night). This is very significant as it helps to position your spirit at a state that enables it to access the pure revelations of the word of God. Sad to say, many who are engaged in ministering the word haven't shown the carefulness and consistency with which they approach meditation of the word and prayers. Some in their meditation moments, have their phones with them, getting distracted with calls, social media, etc. Yet, they want to be granted access into the mysteries of the word. They fail to realize that God by His Spirit is the only one capable of granting a man access into the mysteries of the Kingdom. Until God and your devotional moments are treated with lots of reverence, understanding the word of God properly will be a witch-hunt: *'Then I saw in the right hand of him who sat on the Throne a scroll with writing* on both sides and sealed with seven seals. And I saw a mighty angel proclaiming in a loud voice, "Who is worthy to break the seals and open the scroll?" But no one in heaven or on earth or under the earth could open the scroll or look inside it. I wept and wept because no one was found who was worthy to open the scroll or look inside. Then one of the elders said to me, "Do not weep! See, the Lion of the tribe of Judah, the Root of David, has triumphed. He is able to open the scroll and its seven seals.'" (Revelation 5:1-5).

'After this I looked, and there before me was a door standing open in heaven. And the voice I had first heard speaking to me like a trumpet said, "Come up here, and I will show you what must take place after this."' (Revelation 4:1)

> **We have to be found worthy of the revelations of God's truth before we are granted access.**

This implies we have to be found worthy of the revelations of God's truth before we are granted access. For God will not give that which is holy to dogs, neither will He cast His pearls (precious stones) to pigs who do not recognize its value and worth (Matthew 7:6). Because ministers have not given their all to be granted access into the truth of His grace, they have taught their own devised theories, feeding the people with *Dos* and *Don'ts*. As such, preventing the people of the genuine breath of God's word, leaving them spiritually empty though they attend church services from Sunday to Sunday. Hence, when the storms of life rage upon these people, they lack what it takes to sustain their faith. This account for the reason why many have backslidden from the faith. Christianity has nothing to do with *Dos* and *Don'ts*, but the revelation of the finished work of the cross —which empowers one to live righteously. This is where the real power over sin is: *"Christ in you, the hope of glory. Christ in you, is the secret of living righteously." (Colossians 1:27)*

Peter the apostle had a proper understanding of the truth of grace when he spoke during a dispute among the believers: *'Then some of the believers who belonged to the party of the Pharisees stood up and said, "The Gentiles must be circumcised and required to keep the law of Moses." The apostles and elders met to consider this question. After much discussion, Peter got up and addressed them: "Brothers, you know that some time ago God made a choice among you that the Gentiles might hear from my lips the message of the gospel and believe. God, who knows the heart, showed that he accepted them by giving the Holy Spirit to them, just as He did to us. He did not discriminate between us and them, for he purified their hearts by faith. Now then, why do you try to test God by putting on the necks of Gentiles a yoke that neither we nor our ancestors have been able to bear? No! We believe it is through the grace of our Lord Jesus that we are saved, just as they are.' (Acts 15:5-11)*

> Being ordained an apostle does not mean you are doctrinally sound. Watch out!

Beloved, in this graceful generation, we are truly free from the yoke of the law. That was Peter's emphasis to the apostles and elders of the

Church. This implies that some of the Church leaders and apostles did not understand the fullness of what Christ death on the cross brought, as they were disputing this truth. The same problem still exists among Church leaders. Being ordained an apostle does not mean you are doctrinally sound. Watch out!

Humility is Acknowledging and Confessing

The challenge many pastors and Church leaders have is the lack of humility to acknowledge their mistakes of wrong teachings over the years. Many have even written books on what they later realized was heretical. But they get overcome by the pride of refusing to correct themselves, as they wonder what people will say. This fear makes them not to acknowledge the truth of their challenges. Paul said something very important: *"Further, my brothers and sisters, rejoice in the Lord! It is no trouble for me to write the same things to you again, and it is a safeguard for you. Watch out for those dogs, those evildoers, those mutilators of the flesh. For it is we who are the circumcision, we who serve God by His Spirit, who boast in Christ Jesus, and who put no confidence in the flesh, though, I myself also have reasons for such confidence. If someone else thinks they have reasons to put confidence in the flesh, I have more: circumcised on the eighth day, of the people of Israel, of the tribe of Benjamin, a Hebrew of Hebrews; in regard to the law, a Pharisee; as for zeal, persecuting the church; as for righteousness based on the law, faultless. But whatever were gains to me I now consider loss for the sake of Christ. What is more, I consider everything a loss because of the surpassing greatness of knowing Christ Jesus my Lord, for whose sake I have lost all things. I consider them garbage that I may gain Christ and be found in him, not having a righteousness of my own that comes from the law, but that which is through faith in Christ, the righteousness that comes from God on the basis of faith." (Philippians 3:1-9)*

Paul came to the point in his life that he publicly acknowledged his wrong. He lived by the law, taught the law, without understanding the true meaning of the message of grace brought by the finished work of the cross. His humility caused him to ascribe his former way of life and doctrine as dung and loss, so that he might be able to embrace the fullness of what Jesus has done. Else, we have no benefit in the redemption package. That explains why many still struggle with sin, as they fail to realize the price for their victory is fully paid. All they need to access this victory is to believe and confess what redemption brought to them, and to walk away from all ungodliness.

Wake-up, Church

Paul, awakening to the beauty of the message of grace, he was appointed the apostle to herald the message to the Gentiles, to reveal to them their acceptance in Christ, and joint heirs with Him because of the finished work of Christ. Paul went everywhere teaching the churches about the glory of the finished work of the cross. At some points, he warned against false teachers. He even rebuked the church in Galatia for not walking according to the message of grace: *"You foolish Galatians! Who has bewitched you? Before your very eyes Jesus Christ was clearly portrayed as crucified. I would like to learn just one thing from you: Did you receive the Spirit by the works of the law, or by believing what you heard? Are you so foolish? After beginning by means of the Spirit, are you now trying to finish by means of the flesh? Have you experienced so much in vain if it really was in vain? So again I ask, does God give you his Spirit and work miracles among you by the works of the law, or by your believing what you heard? So also Abraham believed God, and it was credited to him as righteousness. Understand, then, that those who have faith are children of Abraham. Scripture foresaw that God would justify the Gentiles by faith, and announced the gospel in advance to Abraham…" (Galatians 3:1-8)*

Hence, it is evident that all attempts to walk by the law is of the flesh. It's a rejection of what Christ did. To live a life pleasing to the Lord must be the focus of every believer. That is what saves, sanctifies, and purifies a person is faith in Jesus and dependence on Him. Christ specified that without Him, one can do nothing (John 15:5). No one can live and walk in righteousness if his reliance is not on Jesus. This must be the center message of every true Christian leader.

No One is above Scriptural Authority

Many leaders have been overtaken by the spirit of error. This is because, instead of depending on the Holy Spirit for understanding as they search the Scriptures, they approach it casually, depending on their intellect. Others have solely listened to preachers without consistently examining the Scriptures to prove the verity of what they heard. The right attitude to have as we listen to teachings, is to respectfully be like the believers in Berea who searched the Scriptures daily to see if Paul's teachings were true (Acts 17:11). It is the responsibility of every believer to verify the certainty of what they have been taught. Verifying is not a sign of rebellion or lack of submission to your leader, as many leaders have accused some of their church members for being rebellious when they tried to verify the certainty of what they were taught.

In relation to verifying and being assured of the certainty of what you have been taught, Luke wrote to Theophilus, a government official; *"Many have undertaken to draw up an account of the things that have been fulfilled among us, just as they were handed down to us by those who from the first were eyewitnesses and servants of the word. With this in mind, since I myself have carefully investigated everything from the beginning, I too decided to write an orderly account for you, most excellent Theophilus, so that you may know the certainty of the things you have been taught." (Luke 1:1-4)*

Luke basically presented the Scriptures to Theophilus as the basis for his assurance of the things he has been taught, and not just the people who taught him. This means irrespective of who you listen to (mentor, spiritual father, pastor), searching the Scriptures to ensure you haven't been taught the wrong thing is appropriate. It is not a dishonor to whoever taught you. Rather it will be more honorable to them when you realize that they taught you the right things. Paul was true to the message and made sure he preserved its authenticity no matter what he was faced with or who he was addressing: *"Then after fourteen years, I went up again to Jerusalem, this time with Barnabas. I took Titus along also. I went in response to a revelation and, meeting privately with those esteemed as leaders, I presented to them the gospel that I preach among the Gentiles. I wanted to be sure I was not running and had not been running my race in vain. Yet not even Titus, who was with me, was compelled to be circumcised, even though he was a Greek. This matter arose because some false believers had infiltrated our ranks to spy on the freedom we have in Christ Jesus and to make us slaves. We did not give in to them for a moment, so that the truth of the gospel might be preserved for you. As for those who were held in high esteem— whatever they were makes no difference to me; God does not show favoritism —they added nothing to my message. On the contrary, they recognized that I had been entrusted with the task of preaching the gospel to the uncircumcised...those esteemed as pillars, gave me and Barnabas the right hand of fellowship when they recognized the grace given to me. They agreed that we should go to the Gentiles, and they to the circumcised." (Galatians 2:1-9)*

Paul being given a right hand of fellowship was an affirmation of the authenticity of the message of grace he was preaching. Though his principal affirmation was his certainty that Jesus by the Holy Spirit revealed these truths to him.

When Peace Finally Comes

When a person's life and teachings align with the teachings of the Gospel, that is when real peace can be experienced: *"For in Christ Jesus neither circumcision availeth anything, nor uncircumcision, but a new creature. And as many as walk according to THIS RULE, peace be on them, and mercy, and upon the Israel of God." (Galatians 6:16)*

The Christian is further admonished: *"Let us therefore, as many as be perfect, be thus minded and if in anyway, ye be otherwise minded, God shall reveal even this unto you. Nevertheless, whereto we have already attained, let us walk by the SAME RULE, let us mind the same thing." (Philippians 3:15-16)*

Those that would experience real peace in their pilgrimage in this world are those who understand this rule — Grace over Law!

CHAPTER 8

The Line Drawn By Grace

~~~

Grace is not Cheap

This is not to say there is a danger in grace. Rather, the way God deals with man in this dispensation of grace might get one into thinking that God is slow to anger. It appears God is quiet when people do wrong, compared to how He dealt with those under the law. In the Old Covenant, if people were caught in immorality, they were to be stoned: *"This woman was taken in adultery, in the very act... Moses in the law commanded us, that such should be stoned." (John 8:4-5)*

Today, sin has become the norm. Worst of it, Christians are perpetually living sinfully and few seem to be bold enough to rebuke them. Yet, God still seems to be quiet. Instead of having a heart broken before God that hates iniquity, we have been programmed to sin and ask for forgiveness; without remorse, nor any intention to quit sinning: *"What shall we say then? Shall we continue in sin, that grace may abound! God forbid..." (Romans 6:1-2)* This implies it is very grievous to despise God's grace, or to take it for granted, by living in sin. The consciousness of grace should cause us to reverence and serve Him: *"And his grace which was bestowed upon me was not in vain; but I labored more abundantly than they all: yet not I, but the grace of God which was with me." (1 Corinthians 15:10)*

Grace does not mean we should become irresponsible and unaccountable as we expect God to do everything for us. No! We are supposed to collaborate with Him. Many have misunderstood the concept of grace. Paul the preacher of grace more than every other apostle, understood what it means to collaborate with the Lord. He labored more than the other apostles with regards to the gospel, ensuring that the message of God's grace appearing to all may go across the world.

The Demands of Grace

By understanding the beauty of grace, it becomes challenging comprehending the standards grace demands for the believer. This is where many have missed it thinking grace is cheap. The introduction of grace by the Lord in this dispensation, was not in any way a lowering of the standard for righteousness and holiness, rather, He was raising the bar. That is why He gave us His grace since by our abilities, we cannot uphold the standards of holiness and righteousness. Jesus emphasized to His disciples: *"Do not think I have come to abolish the Law or the Prophets; I have not come to abolish them but to fulfil them. For truly I tell you, until heaven and earth disappear, not the smallest letter, not the least stroke of a pen, will by any means disappear from the Law until everything is accomplished. Therefore anyone who sets aside one of the least of these commands and teaches others accordingly will be called least in the kingdom of heaven, but whoever practices and teaches these commands will be called great in the kingdom of heaven. For I tell you that unless your righteousness surpasses that of the Pharisees and the teachers of the law, you will certainly not enter the kingdom of heaven."* (Matthew 5:17-20)

Jesus emphasized this to His disciples because when one hears the beauties of grace, one may not easily notice the demands it sets for the believer. In fact, one would rather be tempted to think the laws have been abolished. That is the reason He had to clarify — *Do not think I have come to abolish the Law or the Prophets!* The Pharisees represented everything about the law. Jesus called to the attention of His disciples that until their righteousness exceed that of the Pharisees and teachers of the law, they will certainly have no part with God's kingdom! From this, it does not appear the standards of righteousness under the law was dropped or lowered for today's dispensation. Rather, it was reinforced. A proof of the bars being raised with regards to righteousness for today's dispensation can be seen in Christ teachings: *"You have heard that it was said, 'You shall not commit adultery.' But I tell you that anyone who looks at a woman lustfully has already committed adultery with her in his heart." (Matthew 5:27-28)*

1. Live in Purity

We are expected to live pure lives and to harbor no traces of ungodliness in our thoughts. Our hearts, thoughts, motives, ought to be sanctified. We cannot experience a genuine relationship with the Lord if our inner-man is not purged: *"For the word of God is alive and active. Sharper than any double-edged sword, it penetrates even to dividing soul and spirit...judges the thoughts and attitudes of the heart."* (Hebrews 4:12). Paul the apostle stressed this point when he wrote to the Church in Thessalonica: *"Do not quench the Spirit...Reject every kind of evil. May God Himself, the God of peace, sanctify you through and through? May your whole spirit, soul and body be kept blameless...The one who calls you is faithful, and he will do it." (1 Thessalonica 5:19-24)*

So, to ensure that the working of the Spirit (a work of grace) in us is not quenched, we must be sanctified on the inside. That's how much the revealed grace of God demands from us!

2. Continue in the Faith

It is grievous for anyone who once experienced the grace of God, to walk away from the faith. It would have been better if they had never experienced it: *"If they have escaped the corruption of the world by knowing our Lord and Savior Jesus Christ and are again entangled in it and are overcome, they are worse off at the end than they were at the beginning. It would have been better for them not to have known the way of righteousness, than to have known it and then to turn their backs on the sacred command that was passed on to them." (2 Peter 2:20-21)*

It bleeds the heart of the Father whenever a person turns away from His grace into a life of disobedience. This is because the Father had to implore His best for the remedy of sin — which is the sacrifice of His Son. He was subjected to such hostility of sinners. Hence, walking away from His grace is like saying it was not necessary for Christ to have died. The Lord punishes that seriously, sentencing those who reject His Son with the lake of fire. There is a level grace that when one experiences, and yet chose to walk away, is considered blasphemy: *"Therefore let us move beyond the elementary teachings about Christ and be taken forward to maturity, not laying again the foundation of repentance from acts that lead to death...It is impossible for those who have once been enlightened, who have tasted the heavenly gift, who have shared in the Holy Spirit, who have tasted the goodness of the word of God and the powers of the coming age and who have fallen away, to be brought back to repentance. To their loss they are crucifying the Son of God all over again and subjecting him to public disgrace." (Hebrews 6:1,4-6)*

The reason why their continuous sinning is considered subjecting the Lord Jesus to public shame is because the testimony of grace about our salvation is a public declaration. That is why Peter said we were called out of darkness to show forth His marvelous light (1 Peter 2:9). Showing forth is a public declaration and profession of faith. That is also what water baptism is, a public declaration that we are dead, buried, and resurrected with Christ! This means true Christianity apart from being a genuine transformation of the heart, must also be accompanied by a daily visible life of sanctification.

> Every time Christians live in compromise, they are doing great damage to the faith, subjecting Jesus Christ to public ridicule.

No doubt, the Scriptures says that the true disciples of Christ will be known by their fruits (visible to all). Therefore, the life of the Christian is as much a public declaration as a heart transformation. This would mean every time Christians live in compromise, they are doing great damage to the faith, subjecting Jesus Christ to public ridicule, thereby, enlisting themselves to the judgment of the Lord. This may be strange, but grace does not rollout the judgment of God. It may hold back judgment for a season,

> "Trespassers will be prosecuted to the full extent of the law!" Signed: The Sisters of Mercy.

but does not totally annul it. It was found on the wall of a private property, "Trespassers will be prosecuted to the full extent of the law!" Signed: The Sisters of Mercy.

3. 'All or Nothing' Rule

The all or nothing rule has to do with total obedience. Grace demands a total walk in Christ. This is because the walk in righteousness is based on relationship with the Lord. Walking by the word in one aspect and not in the rests is disobedience to the Lord, as the same Lord set the standards for all: *'For whosoever keeps the whole law and yet stumbles at just one point is guilty of breaking all of it. For he who said, "You shall not commit adultery," also said, "You shall not murder."'* (James 2:10-11)

It is either all or nothing. This is realized by letting the Lord lead you. That is why Jesus summarized all the laws into love for the Father and for mankind: *"Jesus replied, 'Love the Lord your God with all your heart and with all your soul and with all your mind.' This is the first and greatest commandment. And the second is like it: 'Love your neighbor as yourself.' All the Law and the Prophets hang on these two commandments."* (Matthew 22:37-40)

Once a person loves the Lord, he or she will not live in a way that displeases Him. So, irrespective of the freedom that grace brings, one has to walk with godly reverence, focusing on Christ, to work out one's salvation with fear and trembling (Philippians 2:12). Bible commands us to abstain from all appearances of evil (1Thessalonians 5:22). For example, you do not go watching porn under the pretext that grace has freed you from sin. Else, you will find yourself in sexual pollution. Watch out!

The concept of *'All or Nothing Rule'* is the reason why Paul when teaching the Church in Galatia, referred to the various aspects of the fruit of the Spirit, rather than presenting them as different fruits: *"But the fruit of the Spirit is joy, peace, patience, kindness, goodness, faithfulness, gentleness, and self-control. Against such there is no law."* (Galatians 5:22-23). By this presentation, it makes us realize that there is only one fruit of the Spirit with different aspects of the fruit. Which means you cannot claim to have the fruit of the Spirit if there is a missing aspect (component) of it in your life. Therefore, if you lack say self-control, you cannot claim to have peace, joy, faithfulness, etc. The same is true for the rest. This would mean when the Holy Spirit works on a person, the evidence will be all the different aspects of the fruit noticeable in the person's life.

> A life which is a sweet aroma before the Lord is that which is pleasing to Him, sanctified, and bears the fruit of the Spirit, as evidence of the working of His Spirit.

This thoroughness of the Spirit's work in us makes our lives and bodies portray real worship to God —a living and pleasing sacrifice acceptable to Him (Romans 12:1). This is also implied by Paul to the Church of Corinth: *"For we are to God the sweet aroma of Christ among those who are being saved..." (2 Corinthians 2:15)*. A life which is a sweet aroma before the Lord is that which is pleasing to Him, sanctified, and bears the fruit of the Spirit, as evidence of the working of His Spirit. That is why on the day of Pentecost (a day the people bring the first fruits of their produce and offers it as a sacrifice to God), the fire came on the heads of the one hundred and twenty disciples (Acts 2:1-4). It was the Lord letting them know that their lives were the firstfruits He wanted sacrificed to Him, and not the offerings of their produce. That is genuine worship —the demands of grace!

4. Walk by Knowledge

Grace demands us to walk by the revealed truth of God's word, and holds us accountable if we do not. Hosea the prophet spoke emphatically concerning this: *"My people are destroyed from lack of knowledge. Because you have rejected knowledge, I also reject you as my priests..."* (Hosea 4:6). James said this another way: *"If anyone, then, knows the good they ought to do and doesn't do it, it is sin for them." (James 4:17)*

God indeed holds this generation accountable because of how far He has gone to bring us knowledge. He did not only send His Son, but also the Holy Spirit to guide us into all truth (John 16:13). Luke emphasized to Theophilus, cautioning him as he walks with the Lord; *"Therefore since we are God's offspring, we should not think that the divine being is like gold or silver or stone an image made by human design and skill. In the past God overlooked such ignorance, but now he commands all people everywhere to repent." (Acts 17:29-30)*

It is undisputed that grace holds a higher standard for us than it did for the people of the Old Covenant. The Lord tolerated certain aspects of sin in the Old Covenant because of the ignorance of the people. But now, with all the provisions He has made for His truth to be freely revealed to man, there is no excuse for lack of knowledge. The condemnation that comes upon those in the graceful generation is not because the Lord is condemning them, but the truth (light) they reject is what brings them condemnation: *"For God so loved the world that he gave his one and only Son, that whoever believes in him shall not perish but have eternal life. For God did not send his Son into the world to condemn the world, but to save the world through him. Whoever believes in him is not condemned, but whoever does not believe stands condemned already because they have not believed in the name of God's one and only Son. This is the verdict: Light has come into the world, but people loved darkness instead of light because their deeds were evil."* (John 3:16-19)

CHAPTER 9

The Dangers of Grace

The Abuse of Grace

The account of Eli the Priest is a typical example of the abuse of God's grace in the Old Covenant: *"And the LORD said to Samuel, Behold I will do a thing in Israel, at which both the ears of every one that heareth it shall tingle. In that day I will perform against Eli all things which I have spoken concerning his house. When I begin, I will also make an end. For I have told him that I will judge his house for ever for the iniquity which he knoweth, because his sons made themselves vile, and he restrained them not." (1Samuel 3:12-13)*

Eli took the grace of God for granted. So, the Lord decided to kill him in a dramatic way. When God brought judgment against him and his sons, it was so serious that when his daughter-in-law heard of their deaths, she had an immediate labor and died in the process of delivery. The child was then named Ichabod, which implies, the glory is departed! (1Samuel 4:19-22). When God's grace on a man comes to an end, the first evidence is the absence of God's glory. Strange things start happening in his life. All the tragedies that happened to Eli and his sons, was evident that the glory had departed. This undoubtedly means God's grace is the radiating glory in a man's life.

This concept of grace and the glory working hand-in-glove is portrayed in the life of Zerubbabel: *"... This is the word of the LORD to Zerubbabel: Not by might nor by power, but by My Spirit, says the LORD of Hosts. What are you; O great mountain? Before Zerubbabel you will become a plain. Then he will bring forth the capstone accompanied by shouts of 'Grace, grace to it!" (Zechariah 4:6-7).* Therefore, when grace abundantly operates in your life, God's glory becomes tangible, and you start to soar with wings as eagles.

How to Know When Grace is Abused

> This demonstrates how grace on a person works —It strips you of everything you can boast of, and rather empowers you with God's life and strength.

It is worth noting that many Christians ignorantly abuse the grace of God on their lives. This is because of the way they live, as they fail to take into consideration the leading of the Spirit of the Lord. Paul the apostle was one man who understood God's grace on a person or on a minister: *"I am crucified with Christ; nevertheless I live, yet not I, but Christ liveth in me and the life which I now live in the flesh I live by the faith of the Son of God (he did not boast of his faith, but that of Jesus Christ), who loved me, and gave himself for me." (Galatians 2:20).* This demonstrates how grace on a person works —It strips you of everything you can boast of, and rather empowers you with God's life and strength. Paul conscious of this reality, emphasized; *"I do not frustrate the grace of God: for if righteousness come by the law, then Christ is dead in vain." (Galatians 2:21)*

By this he implies that righteousness is not by the law, but by grace. Living a righteous life, requires one to be more conscious of grace, which has already been manifested in us by the Spirit, from the time one received salvation by accepting the Lord Jesus: *"For by grace are ye saved through faith; and that not of yourselves; it is the gift of God: Not of works, lest any man should boast." (Ephesians 2:8-9)*

Unfortunately, most Christians, even pastors are unaware of the dynamics of grace. This is one of the priceless gifts of God to man which has been over abused. As such, many go through unnecessary experiences; stress, defeats, etc. To identify when one is abusing grace, look for the following (as extrapolated from the story of Eli the priest):

i) Making Light of God's Instructions

It should be noted that Eli the priest made light of God's instructions, principles, sacrificial offerings, and would not give it all the reverence due. It is said of him, *"So why do you scorn my sacrifices and offerings?" (1 Samuel 2:29)*. Many Christians today make light of spiritual things as they compromise the Christian values. That is why sin has characterized both the pulpits and pews.

When you find yourself in compromise, it is not the time to give excuses, neither to see it as common within Christendom. Rather, it is time to vehemently reconsider your ways and to stand your ground in Christ, as you fight against it: *"Wherefore let him that thinketh he standeth take heed lest he fall. Hence, your responsibility as Christian in such moments is to shun from sin and all forms of compromise." (1 Corinthians 10:12)*

ii. Honoring Persons at the Expense of Divine Standards

The way Eli treated his sons when they were defiling the sacrifices and offerings was unacceptable. The Lord rebuked him pertaining to this, *"... Why do you honor your sons more than me?"*

(1 Samuel 2:29). As we study the Scriptures, we realize that God is a respecter of nobody but His word, as He has exalted His word above His name (Psalms 138:2). By exalting His word above His name, means His personality only goes in the direction of His word. He expects us as well to exalt and to esteem His word and virtues above everyone else. When we do fail to do that, then we abuse His word and grace, thereby attracting His indignation. This is not to say we should dishonor man or His servants. No! That will attract judgment to our lives also. But in our honor of man, we need to give the credit to the Lord, giving Him all the glory.

iii. Walking in Continuous Disobedience

Notice that the Lord continuously warned Eli, but he would not respond: *"I have warned him continually that judgment is coming upon his family, because his sons are blaspheming God and he has not disciplined them." (1 Samuel 3:13)* One of the ways in which we abuse the grace of God is when we continuously fail to respond accordingly to the demands of His word. Such a continuous act of disobedience will cause us to have a reprobate mind —when we are no longer convicted of sin. Eli seemingly got to this point. The Lord also used a third party (Samuel) to warn him, yet he did not repent of his sin. Rather, his response was shocking —no remorse for his negligence to the work of the Lord: *"Then the LORD said to Samuel, I am about to do something in Israel at which the ears of all who hear it will tingle. On that day I will carry out against Eli everything I have spoken about his family, from beginning to end. I told him that I will judge his house forever for the iniquity of which he knows, because his sons blasphemed God and he did not restrain them. Therefore, I have sworn to the house of Eli, 'The iniquity of Eli's house shall never be atoned for by sacrifice or offering.'" (1 Samuel 3:11-14)*. The next day Eli asked Samuel what the Lord had told him. Samuel was afraid to tell him. Eli called God's judgment on Samuel if he hides from him anything the Lord had told him. *"So, Samuel told Eli everything; he did not hold anything back. 'It is the LORD'S will,' Eli replied, 'Let him do what he thinks best.'" (1 Samuel 3:18)*.

As a priest, his role was to intercede for the people to hold back the judgment of God. Yet, he refused to intercede for his family, he lost the passion for ministry, lost his reverence for God. God departed from him, and the grace also departed. This led to his awful death. The Scriptures demands of us even in our weaknesses to have a repentant heart before the Lord: *"Blessed is the man who is always reverent, but he who hardens his heart falls into trouble." (Proverbs 28:14)*

iv. A Decrease of His Presence Through One's Life

> When a person becomes careless about his relationship with the Lord and his devotion to the ministry the Lord has entrusted him with, then spiritual encounters with the Lord ceases.

This is very crucial. Examining the testimony of Eli from the period he was indifferent about the state of spiritual matters, one sees he stopped having encounters with God: *"...Now in those days messages from the LORD were very rare, and visions were quite uncommon" (1 Samuels 3:1).* When a person becomes careless about his relationship with the Lord and his devotion to the ministry the Lord has entrusted him with, then spiritual encounters with the Lord ceases. Hence, the flow of divine presence through him as before greatly diminishes. The joy of the Lord and the joy of serving Him fades away. Heaven then finds the individual unfit for the assignment of the Lord as long as he will not repent. The Bible is big on this: *"Give not that which is holy to the dogs, neither cast ye your pearls before swine, lest they trample them under their feet..." (Matthew 7:6).* Such individuals may still see gleams of results, may still be able to teach the Scriptures to an appreciable extent, but the anointing and grace that makes the teachings impactful is gone.

> Compromise hinders the continual flow of His presence through us, as well as causes His gifts in us to gradually become dormant and irrelevant.

This does not mean that compromise to spiritual matters will take away the gifts God has freely given to us, for the gifts and calling of God are without repentance (Romans 11:29). That is, God does not take back that which He has already given to us, though we may experience diminishing returns as we try to make use of them. That is why Eli (though he was already likely been rejected by God by this time), could still prophesy to Hannah that her request for a male child has been granted. She then conceived for the first time, though barren, and gave birth to Samuel (1 Samuel 1:12-20). Compromise hinders the continual flow of His presence through us, as well as causes His gifts in us to gradually become dormant and irrelevant. It will hinder us from being granted insights into the deep spiritual matters of the Spirit, as they can only be discerned spiritually (1 Corinthians 2:14). This is a call for us to shun every ungodly lifestyle, then we would automatically gain access into an undeniable divine flow of God's grace and His presence.

CHAPTER 10

Provision of a Door of Escape

God's Grace in Temptations

How glorious it is to live with the consciousness of the availability of God's abundant grace. This dynamic grace of God can be seen in our encounters with temptations:

"There hath no temptation taken you but such as is common to man: but God is faithful, who will not suffer you to be tempted above that ye are able; but will with the temptation also make a way to escape, that ye may be able to bear it." (1Corinthians 10:13).

"The Lord knoweth how to deliver the godly out of temptations..." (2 Peter 2:9)

Concerning dealing with temptations, it is interesting to know that His grace is available for our rescue. One thing to know is that temptations are never from God, but from our heart disposition to the enticement the devil presents before us: *"Let no man say when he is tempted, I am tempted of God: for God cannot be tempted with evil, neither tempted he any man. But every man is tempted, when he is drawn away of his own lust, and enticed?" (James 1:13-14)*

Yet, God takes upon Himself the responsibility to work out for the favor of man an avenue to escape the plans of the devil through the temptations. This therefore is a guarantee to us that there is no temptation we will face beyond our ability to bear, and without God being able to empower us to be victorious over. What a grace! Therefore, the issue of temptation is no longer a big deal to the Christian who has fully submitted his heart to the Lord.

The Expected Mindset of the Christian

> Your mindset will be a determining factor if you will find strength in God's word in the hour of temptation, irrespective of the intensity of the temptation.

Having examined the grace of God which always manifest when a Christian faces temptation, there is every reason for this grace not to be taken for granted. Therefore, the Christian ought to have the right mindset when faced with temptation. Your mindset will be a determining factor if you will find strength in God's word in the hour of temptation, irrespective of the intensity of the

> We need to have a positive mindset in the face of temptation, not seeing it as a vulnerable moment, but as an opportunity for us to proof the firmness and certainty of our loyalty to the Lord and His word.

temptation. Many Christians who yielded to temptations were not because they were above them to bear, but they had the wrong mindsets. Others faced with temptations have turned away from the faith. We need to have a positive mindset in the face of temptation, not seeing it as a vulnerable moment, but as an opportunity for us to proof the firmness and certainty of our loyalty to the Lord and His word. It is rather unfortunate to say that many who see temptations as moments of vulnerability, already have their excuses prepared to give for bowing to them as soon as they present themselves. The Bible tells us, *"My brethren, count it all joy when ye fall into diverse temptations; Knowing this, that the trying of your faith worketh patience." (James 1:2-3)* This mindset is reinforced in one of the epistles of Peter when he wrote: *"So be truly glad. There is wonderful joy ahead, even though you must endure many trials for a little while. These trials will show that your faith is genuine…" (1 Peter 1:6-7)*

> Many who see temptations as moments of vulnerability, already have their excuses prepared to give for bowing to them as soon as they present themselves.

> The mindset of refusal to yield to temptation no matter the intensity of it, works in us a profound glory.

The mindset of refusal to yield to temptation no matter the intensity of it, works in us a profound glory. Therefore, we should never have a defeatist mentality when we encounter temptations. We should instead build a positive attitude. This gives us the confidence to declare the word of God at the face of it, so as to counteract the temptation. Temptations are there so we may put faith to work, hence, a blessing when we refuse to yield, *"Blessed is the man that endureth temptation" (James 1:12).* As we grasp these truths about our attitudes and mindsets when dealing with temptations, it ushers us into the state of rests and no worries in our Christian pilgrimage. Paul the apostle said about himself, *"Serving the Lord with all humility of mind, and with many tears, and temptations, which befall me..."* *(Acts 20:19).* He considered the encounter of manifold temptations as one of the very essential ways of proving his love and service to God. This must be true with us. Without the right mindset at the face of temptations, you will again become vulnerable to sins you once gained victory over.

> Without the right mindset at the face of temptations, you will again become vulnerable to sins you once gained victory over.

Characteristics of Temptation

Everyone faces temptation. Just as we all have different strengths, interests, and weaknesses, we also have different areas we could be tempted in. Some might be easily enticed to tell lies, steal, or gamble, while others are easily lured to smoke, fornicate, etc. What entices one person may have no effect on the other. When a person has difficulties resisting a particular act of sin, he then concludes, "This is just the way I am!" He then gives himself over to it. After repeatedly yielding to the act of sin, it becomes normal to him as he ceases to see the wrong in it. That is a dangerous state to be in. It is important to note that all temptations are based on a fantasy. It starts with a thought. However, simply thinking about something does not automatically mean that you have sinned. As you harbor the thought, your imagination begins to take over, "I wonder how it would be to have this, sleep with this person, etc." As you imagine what the experience might be like, a strong desire for it then steps in and grows. At that point, it becomes an inner battle choosing to either turn away from the temptation or consent to it, and sooner or later, the flesh starts longing to be gratified with it.

> Temptation is an enticement to go beyond the safety and fulfilling boundaries set by God.

God created us with legitimate needs and desires. He intended for those legitimate desires to be met within certain parameters of His word and values. Achieving that desire beyond the parameter of His word becomes sinful and destructive. Hence, God establishing limits is not to prevent us from having fun or enjoying life, but in order to protect us. Temptation is an enticement to go beyond the safety and fulfilling boundaries set by God. For example, He certainly gave us the appetite for

> Our freedom ends where God has placed restrictions.

food; otherwise, we would die of hunger. But if we allow our appetite go past the boundary of self-control, we over-eat and become gluttonous. That becomes a sin and can affect our health. Similarly, the desire for sex is a gift from God, but must only be engaged in the context of marriage for it to be right. Our freedom ends where God has placed restrictions.

With this understanding, we must be on our guard, for Satan is going around like a roaring lion looking for those to destroy. And his strategy is through temptation. Even Jesus, because He was also fully man, was tempted in all things as we are, but was without sin (Hebrews 4:15). How wonderful it is to know that we never face a temptation that Jesus Himself did not face. And since He sinned not, then we too can resist bowing to it.

How Not to Yield to Temptation

The enemy (Satan) always tries to narrow our focus on something minuscule — the object of temptation. Satan tempting Jesus to bow down and worship him so he gives Him the whole world (Matthew 4:8-11), he tried to narrow His attention to the glory of getting the whole world. That's exactly what he still does today, as he keeps succeeding to make many to fall. He tricks couples to see the pleasure they will get having sex with someone else, without pointing them to the possible consequences amongst others — like losing their marriage. Our heavenly Father, on the other hand, desires that we keep sight on the big picture, which is the beauty of resisting the pressure to sin, and the glorious reward that follows.

These ways will help you to resist the promptings to sin:

i). Ask Yourself Questions

Before you act, consider the answers to the following: Is this thing something I really need or its just a mere desire? If I should yield to this temptation, what will be the immediate and future consequences to me and those around me? Am I prepared to endure the consequences no matter how grievous it may be? Is there a better way to get this need met without sinning? What do I gain yielding?

ii). Identify Areas of Weaknesses

> Making straight paths for your feet reduces the probability of vulnerability to temptation.

Most people have one or more vulnerabilities. Be mindful of places, or situations that might foster temptations, and avoid them: *"Blessed is the man that walketh not in the counsel of the ungodly, nor standeth in the way of sinners, nor sitteth in the seat of the scornful." (Psalms 1:1)* It is interesting to know that there are paths and seats considered as ungodly. Making straight paths for your feet reduces the probability of vulnerability to temptation. This approach reduces the chances of certain weaknesses having the opportunity to manifest. The Scripture is clear on this when it says you should not give a foothold to the devil (Ephesians 4:27).

iii). Meditate on the Word

> Prayerfully meditating on the word consistently kills the tendency to easily give in to temptation.

This is very necessary. David said, *"Thy word have I hidden in my heart that I might not sin against you" (Psalms 119:11).* Prayerfully meditating on the word consistently kills the tendency to easily give in to temptation.

iv). Declare What the Word Says

This is a very powerful tool in overcoming the promptings to sin. When the evil thought gets into your mind, quickly begin to declare to yourself what the Scriptures say. That emboldens you on the inside as it makes you see that act of sin as very sinful. Hence, every desire for it fades away. That was exactly what Jesus did when the tempted came to Him, tempting Him to sin. Jesus kept declaring, *"It is written!" (Matthew 4:1-11).* His response of *"It is written,"* was not principally to the devil, as much as it was a means of empowering Himself not to bow to the promptings and enticements of sin.

V). Be Accountable to a Friend

Select a confidential, trustworthy brother or sister in Christ who loves your well-being and is spiritual. There is nothing as strengthening and encouraging to the soul like a friend checking on you to know how you are fairing. Being sincere and accountable to that person about your daily struggles will be of great help to you. The consciousness that you mess up, this person will know because you are accountable to him or her, will greatly help you to an extent in resisting the temptation.

vi). Rely on the Holy Spirit

This is key. Once you rely on Him, He will lead and direct you in ways that will preserve you. Jesus taught the disciples that when they pray, they should ask the Lord not to lead them into temptation (Matthew 6:13). That is to say, He should direct their path in ways that do not get them to a place where they would yield to the promptings of the flesh.

CHAPTER 11

Reinforcing The New Covenant

This is very important because many people live without the consciousness of the New Covenant and its benefits to them. It is the responsibility of the minister to reawaken the consciousness of it in the hearts of the people. This can only be done by means of teachings. Nothing can influence a person's mind like information. Just because Christ came and died and enacted a New Covenant, does not mean that people do live in the New Covenant. There are several Christians who still live in the Old Covenant. As a result, the beauty of redemption is not evident in their lives. Paul commanded the Roman Christians to be transformed by the renewal of their minds (Romans 12:2).

Transitioning to the New Covenant

The minister is supposed to have a thorough understanding of the Old Covenant, the biblical background of the Old Covenant period, customs and cultures of Bible times, types (things which were being done in the Old Covenant as a shadow of the reality to be revealed in the New Covenant), the New Covenant reality of the types, and the teachings of Christ. This will help him to fully understand the transition. Failure to understand the New Covenant reality, he will keep practicing the Old Covenant types thinking it is present truth. This is where many ministers are lacking. With the lack of proper understanding about the transition from the Old to the New, they have treated both covenants inappropriately. They see the New Covenant as an addition to the Old Covenant instead as a transition from it. This can be seen in the things they preach and teach.

What will be of great help in understanding this transition, will be to acquaint oneself with the operations and teachings of Christ, examining His conflicts with the Pharisees (teachers of the law), and how He addressed issues about their doctrines. We are admonished to follow in His footsteps: *"Those who say they live in God should live their lives as Jesus did." (1 John 2:6).* Once these have been taken care of, then the lives we live will reveal our understanding and appreciation for that which Jesus accomplished on that ancient cross.

The Focus of the Minister

The focus of the minister with regards to what to teach the church is of great importance. When you read the entire Bible, you will immediately notice that God has always interacted with mankind differently, depending on the dispensation. We now live in a dispensation of grace, brought to us by the sacrifice of Christ. He is our standard and should be the only focus. The minister should focus on the person of Christ and the entire redemption package He made available for the believer: *"Therefore every teacher of the law who has become a disciple in the kingdom of heaven is like the owner of a house who brings out of his storeroom new treasures as well as old." (Matthew 13:52)* A disciple in the kingdom of heaven means one who has been discipled in the teachings of Christ (the New Covenant). Bringing from his storeroom new treasures — talks of the redemption package, and old treasures — talks of the things of the Old Covenant that still stand the test of the New Covenant revelation. This is how a minister should approach the Bible. He should focus on bringing the New Covenant truth of the finished work of the cross, and his preaching from the Old Testament should be in light of the New Testament. This is very necessary if he intends to build a Christ-centered people, who know how to live in their divine authority.

> The more focus and attention is given to the Old Covenant as opposed to the New Covenant, the more people remain blind to the New Covenant realities.

Unfortunately, many ministers have not done so. Most of their teachings do focus on the Old Covenant. Most often because the Old Testament is very dramatic, full of stories, meanwhile the New Testament is more revelatory. It takes more of an intimate relationship with Christ to fall in love and better appreciate the New Testament, as opposed to the Old Testament. So, most Christians love to hear preaching from the Old Testament as they find it very dramatic. What they and the ministers do not know is that the more focus and attention is given to the Old Covenant as opposed to the New

Covenant, the more people remain blind to the New Covenant realities: *"Now if the ministry that brought death, which was engraved in letters on stone, came with glory, so that the Israelites could not look steadily at the face of Moses because of its glory, transitory though it was, will not the ministry of the Spirit be even more glorious? If the ministry that brought condemnation was glorious, how much more glorious is the ministry that brings righteousness! For what was glorious has no glory now in comparison with the surpassing glory. And if what was transitory came with glory, how much greater is the glory of that which lasts! Therefore, since we have such a hope, we are very bold. We are not like Moses, who would put a veil over his face to prevent the Israelites from seeing the end of what was passing away. But their minds were made dull, for to this day the same veil remains when the old covenant is read. It has not been removed, because only in Christ is it taken away. Even to this day when Moses is read, a veil covers their hearts. But whenever anyone turns to the Lord, the veil is taken away."* (2 Corinthians 3:7-16)

The Ministries of Death and Righteousness

The teaching of the Old Covenant is talked of as the ministry that brings death, while the teaching of the New Covenant is seen as the ministry that brings righteousness, which is much glorious. Every minister ought to be properly schooled and discipled in the teachings of the New Testament. Their teachings and preaching must focus more on that. This will bring the people into a surpassing glory as they begin to understand the things freely given to them by Christ. The glory of the Old Covenant from teaching the law was very temporal. Jesus became the culmination (end) of the law so that righteousness is made possible for all who believes in Him (Romans 10:4).

> It is a ministry of righteousness only when the teachings are in line with the life and teachings of Christ.

Though many others may teach from the New Testament, it does not automatically make it a ministry of righteousness. It is a ministry of righteousness only when the teachings are in line with the life and teachings of Christ. Emphasis must be on the person of Christ, His works, and His teachings. For Jesus is the radiance of the invisible God, the full expression of the Godhead (Hebrews 1:3), and the completion of the saints (Colossians 2:10).

Dimensions in Grace

> As we grow in our relationship and knowledge of Christ, we gain access into a greater sphere of possibilities in Him.

There are dimensions in expressions of the grace of God. This does not mean there are multiple graces. These dimensions can be experienced by growing in grace. Growth in grace comes about by our increase in knowledge of Jesus Christ: *"But grow in the grace and knowledge of our Lord and Savior Jesus Christ…" (2 Peter 3:18)* Jesus is the definition of God's grace. As we grow in our

> It impossible to benefit of the fullness of grace without an increased intimacy with Jesus.

relationship and knowledge of Christ, we gain access into a greater sphere of possibilities in Him. It is evident from the Scriptures that they that know their God shall be strong and do great exploits (Daniel 11:32). This makes it impossible to benefit of the fullness of grace without an increased intimacy with Jesus.

This is what every pastor and all those involved in teaching God's people must be more concerned with—bringing teachings that ignites passion for wanting to know Christ more. This will enable the people to grow to the point where God's grace will be evident in their lives. This is because of increase in their intimacy with the Lord Jesus and increase in the richness of His word in them.

The Strangeness of the New Covenant to Angels

Isaiah the prophet saw the uniqueness of the New Covenant, and the challenges the people will have believing it. That is why he cried out: *"Who has believed our message and to whom has the arm of the LORD been revealed?" (Isaiah 53:1)* Once the beauty of the New Covenant is not received, its benefits will not be experienced. Jesus is the end of the Law only to those who have come to Him in repentance and for salvation. Only such people can experience the freedom He brings. The uniqueness of the New Covenant with its packages is such that angels desire to look into it: *"Concerning this salvation, the prophets, who spoke of the grace that was to come to you, searched intently and with the greatest care, trying to find out the time and circumstances to which the Spirit of Christ in them was pointing when he predicted the sufferings of the Messiah and the glories that would follow. It was revealed to them that they were not serving themselves but you, when they spoke of the things that have now been told you by those who have preached the gospel to you by the Holy Spirit sent from heaven. Even angels long to look into these things." (1 Peter 1:10-12)*

> The peak of spiritual encounters is not when one sees angelic manifestations, nor when one is caught up in some heavenly realms (though necessary), but when one understands and live by the revelation of the person of Christ and the grace He freely offers.

From this text, it is evident that angels do not understand the fullness of the mystery of grace. This is so because the revelation of grace was never revealed to them, neither have they ever experienced it, as it was never intended for them. The transition from the Old Covenant to the New was only for man, and not angels. Angels did not experience any transition because it was not about them. This explains the fact that the peak of spiritual encounters is not when one sees angelic manifestations, nor when one is caught up in some heavenly

> The believer will do more exploits understanding the revelation of Christ and His grace, than just seeing an angel.

realms (though necessary), but when one understands and live by the revelation of the person of Christ and the grace He freely offers. It is important to note that the believer will do more exploits understanding the revelation of Christ and His grace, than just seeing an angel. The most angels can do is to be ministering spirits for the saints—the heirs of salvation (Hebrews 1:14). That is, to carry out any service the Lord has for them per time for the sake of the saints. They are mere servants and do not even reason with God on whatever they are assigned to do. Their opinions are not consulted. Only man has the ability to reason with God on any issue, to question God on an issue and be entitled for God to respond, as well as whether he is willing to engage in what God demands or not (though his disobedience to God's instructions may come with consequences). The Bible makes this clear: *"Come now, and let us reason together," Says the LORD, "...If you are willing and obedient, You shall eat the good of the land." (Isaiah 1:18-19)*

Angels have no choice but to do what the Lord wants of them. Any disobedience on their part cannot be forgiven nor atoned for. They do not fall under such category of those to experience God's mercy. Jude pointed to this reality when he wrote, *"And the angels who did not keep their own domain, but abandoned their proper abode, He has kept in eternal bonds under darkness for the judgment of the great day." (Jude 1:6)*. Whereas man can seat on a table with God and present his opinion on a subject — reasoning together with God! Isaiah the prophet made reference to this when he said, *"'Present your case," says the LORD. "Submit your arguments," says the King of Jacob.' (Isaiah 41:21).* This is a great privilege accorded to man and must not be abused or taken for granted.

Other books of Dr. Willibroad W. Ticha

- The Journey
- Cultivating the Spirit of Leadership
- Leadership At Its Best (As Exemplified by the Life and Ministry of Christ)
- The Battle of the Eye (Overcoming the Power of Seduction)
- Dealing With The Esau Syndrome, Killer of Destinies
- Understanding and Interpreting Dreams and Visions
- Reclaiming Yourself from Emotional Trauma
- Fatherhood (The Peak of Leadership)
- Recovering Your Anointing
- Uncovering Misconceptions and Understanding the Truth on Spiritual Warfare.
- The Man Approved by God
- Winning Evangelism (The Believers Manual To Passionate Soul-Winning)

For more information on these or other books by Dr. Willibroad Ticha, contact our office on:

Email: gospelheroes18@gmail.com

YOUTUBE

Please subscribe and hit the notification button for uplifting teachings:

GospelHeroes TV

INSTAGRAM

Please subscribe also to our Instagram: *Dr. Willibroad_*

FACEBOOK

Please follow us on Facebook at: *Dr. Willibroad*

OUR MENTORSHIP PROGRAM

To enroll into our mentorship program (Gospel Heroes Commission International) so as to become a cutting-edge leader, register through the website or send us an email using the following respectively:

Register: *www.tichawillibroad.com/ghci*

Email to: *gospelheroes18@gmail.com*